Perry Block
arraignment
267-3424

The Mountain of My Fear

The Mountain of My Fear

DAVID ROBERTS

THE VANGUARD PRESS, INC.
NEW YORK

Left to right: Matt Hale, Don Jensen, Dave Roberts, Ed Bernd at the start of the climb.

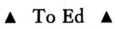 To Ed ▲

Upon the mountains of my fear I climb:
Above, a breakneck scorching rock; no caves,
No col, no water . . . .

▲ Contents

Illustrations

7.   Ed Bernd belaying at the top of the 38th pitch, having just traversed a steep snow-ice slope, on the summit day.

8.   Sunrise on the summit of Mt. Huntington. Left to right: Bernd, Roberts, Hale.

9.   Looking back at the summit and the summit ridge on the descent. The left-hand edge is heavily corniced. Note the steps and fixed rope.

10.   The author, just three pitches below the summit, on the descent.

11.   Ed Bernd rappelling off the Nose on the descent. Note fixed line with loops left on the pitch.

MAPS (*by John Leinung*)

The Mountain of My Fear

1 ▲ The Mountain

The mountain had been there a long time.

If we could define its beginning, perhaps we would place it in the Jurassic age, when several cataclysmic faults thrust the granite core of the Alaska Range into the sky. After that time the mountain may have looked much as it does now. But we must imagine as legacy to the violence of those faults only voiceless eons spent in the silent wear of ice and wind; for the mountain stood one hundred and thirty million years before man would walk upright on some tropical plain. We must imagine an emptiness of time that can be matched only by the emptiness of space: ages explored only by the dark wind that must always have been there, silence broken only by the occasional clatter of a rock set loose in the brief summer thaw, or the wet hiss of an afternoon avalanche.

But a similar history belongs to any mountain, and the rounded Appalachian hills are far more ancient than Alaska's giants. Mount Huntington is remarkable not for its past, but for its present. For the sixty years men have known about it (not many men either), it has possessed a quality common to only a few mountains in the world. A sense of arrested grace, perhaps; a sculptured frailty too savage for any sculptor's hand; a kinship with the air around it that makes it seem always in motion—but these are only metaphors, unable to capture the essence of the mountain. And though we might presume it has no essence, knowing that time will wear it beyond the bone to a heap of detritus, knowing that it cannot outlive the sun, still we are sure that any man's lifetime can span but one flaking of its skin, and that the mountain, doomed as surely as the earth, still possesses something like the earth's persistence, something alien enough from man to partake of a universe he wished he could own.

It is impossible to determine which man first saw Huntington. The Indians, who gave a worshipful name to McKinley (they called it Denali, "the Great One"), made little distinction among the masses that surround it. Since they never got into the heart of the range, none of them may have ever seen Mount Huntington.

But they named the river that comes from the glacier that Huntington heads; and the name, Tokositna ("the river that comes from the land where there are no trees"), suggests that they were familiar with the river's origins, if not the glacier's. Perhaps some hunter, chasing a caribou herd toward the highlands, crossed the tundra hills one day in late summer to see the dirty tongue of the glacier stretch back before him into the bewildering chaos of rock and ice that fringed Denali; perhaps he glimpsed in that chaos a peak or a ridge of what would come to be called Mount Huntington. It couldn't have been more than a glimpse. On a clear day, it is true, one can see Huntington from points in the southern lowlands more than a hundred miles away; but it takes a sharp eye to discriminate its slender peak from the hulking mass of McKinley behind it. No one unaware of the intricate wanderings of the glaciers in the heart of the range could tell that what he saw was a separate mountain, much less a beautiful, virtually unique one.

It remained for the first mountaineers, whose goal was McKinley itself, to approach Huntington. Dr. Frederick Cook, the sadly infamous explorer whose fraudulent claims not only to have stood on the summit of McKinley in 1906, but to have reached the North Pole two years later, obscured his genuine accomplishments, led the first party to explore the Ruth Glacier. At the end of his trek, perhaps only a day or two before he photographed his friend Edward Barrille on the top of a minor peak he would pass off as the highest point in North America, he may have glimpsed Huntington's ice-ribbed northern wall across the glacier's great amphitheater. Four years later Belmore Browne explored the northwest branch of the Ruth to its headwall, passing directly beneath that fluted face in a hopeless effort to climb McKinley from the south (something that was not done until 1954). On July 24 he named the graceful mass of ice and rock that loomed over his tracks after the president of the American Geographical Society, Archer Milton Huntington, who had helped sponsor their trip.

Later that year a group of unsystematic sourdoughs discovered that the key to McKinley was in its northeast flank, and in 1913 the summit was finally reached from that side. For twenty years afterward there seemed to be little point in repeating the exploit; the interests of mountaineers had not yet turned to the lower but beautiful and difficult mountains and routes. Height was the only criterion, and the highest thirty or forty mountains in the world, all in the Himalayas, had still not been climbed. When interest in Alaska returned, it concentrated on McKinley; the northeast route, moreover, seemed the only one possible. Men began to fly near the mountains, but their wary approaches left the smaller mountains too distant to reveal their splendors. Eyes riveted on the hulk of McKinley (a mountain bigger than Everest or Aconcagua or Mont Blanc) scarcely had time to examine the mere 12,240-foot tower of Huntington.

Until 1951, indeed, all that had been accomplished in

the range were six ascents of McKinley (all by the original Muldrow route) and the first ascent of Mount Foraker, the second highest mountain in the region. But one man had, since his undergraduate days at Harvard in the early thirties, climbed and photographed these mountains with a quenchless interest. Bradford Washburn had managed to talk some of the best Alaskan bush pilots into flying right next to the gigantic walls of the McKinley Range. Using the photos from these flights at first only for the sake of planning climbs, he amassed over the years probably the finest collection of mountain pictures in the world. Washburn, born too late to have invented Alaskan mountaineering, should be called its greatest figure. His brilliant schemes seem so sensible today that it is difficult to imagine what boldness they took twenty years ago, his planning so thorough and careful that among some twenty different Alaskan expeditions he seems never to have led a failure. For two decades Washburn made one first ascent after another, not only in the McKinley area, but in the Chugach, St. Elias, Hayes, and Fairweather ranges. He was the first man to climb McKinley three times. He was the first, in 1951, to succeed on it by any route other than the Muldrow, when he led the now-classic first ascent of the West Buttress. Once, in the St. Elias Range, he and Bob Bates had to make a forced march more than a hundred miles out to civilization, low on food; but they traversed 17,000-foot Mount Lucania (making its first ascent) simply because it was in their way. Now director of the Museum of Science in Boston, Washburn still has the ageless, hawk-faced look that glares out of the summit photos of his youth. With an impatient dynamism if anything enhanced by age, he urges mountaineers all over the world to climb in Alaska, knowing they will supersede his own accomplishments. But Washburn, strong-willed, dogmatic, has no time for nostalgia: "Now that route on Foraker's simply *begging* to be done—no question about it, the best thing left in the range." Every expedition that goes to Alaska owes something to his experience. His generosity with advice, praise, and access to his photos has, more than any other factor, encouraged Alaskan mountaineering in the post-Washburn generation. But he cannot rest content to know this. Through his clear, proud eyes speaks the urge for just one more try, the sad knowledge that climbing, like life, is one of those things you can never get enough of.

It was Washburn's pictures, far more than the one that had appeared in Browne's *The Conquest of Mount McKinley,* that made climbers first pay attention to Huntington. Flying by its northwest ridge, which seemed to offer the only hope for Huntington's ascent, Washburn in the late fifties took a series of pictures that captured the mountain's incredible sharpness, its slender symmetry, projected not against the flattening backdrop of McKinley but against the limitless vista of lower peaks, glaciers, and tundra to the south. Primarily through these photographs, Huntington became known as Alaska's hidden prize. A limited attempt in 1957 by several Americans on the northwest ridge convinced them of the difficulty of the huge snow towers that studded this knife-edged route, problems which, because of time and supplies, they could not even begin to attack. In the 1962 *American Alpine Journal,* Washburn indicated briefly what sort of attack he felt would have the best chance of subduing the mountain. But not until 1964 did a full-scale effort assault Huntington.

The idea, one he had long cherished, was Lionel Terray's. Washburn had sent photos of the mountain to Terray, the most famous French climber of his time and perhaps the greatest expedition mountaineer who ever lived. In the spring of 1964, with the support of the French Alpine Club, Terray and seven of his countrymen, all outstanding alpinists, flew to Alaska with the ambitious plan of climbing Huntington, a new and extremely difficult route on McKinley, and a new route on Foraker, all in one summer. That they had underestimated Huntington quickly became apparent to them. In addition, they ran into an extraordinarily cold and stormy May. After two weeks of determined effort on the northwest ridge, they were still far from the summit, cold and demoralized. In addition, Terray had seriously injured his shoulder in a near-fatal accident and was forced to direct the attack from a low snow cave. But with fine tenacity, the expedition kept at it. At last, on May 25, two of them stood in a biting wind on Huntington's summit, the first men ever to reach it. The next day the other six, including Terray, who could use only one arm but had gamely insisted on continuing, were also able to get to the top, following the ropes left by their friends. The victory was a sweet one, but its arduous severity left the men in no mood to attempt their other objectives. They flew out from the Ruth Glacier a few days later. For Terray, it was to be the last great mountain he would ever climb, the last achievement in a career that stretched back beyond the already legendary Annapurna ascent in 1950. He was killed on an unimportant cliff in southern France, with Marc Martinetti, also a Huntington veteran, on a sunny day in September 1965 when, for some unknown reason, the two of them fell, still roped together, 1,200 feet to their death.

Usually after its first ascent a mountain passes into a period of disregard. Perhaps fifty Americans had had their eyes on Huntington before the French succeeded in climbing it; none of them felt much desire now simply to repeat their route, especially since there were so many other good climbs left in Alaska.

One of the people who had wanted to do Huntington was Don Jensen. Don had grown up near San Francisco, where he had learned to love the outdoors. As early as he could remember, his parents had taken his older brother and him on long hiking and camping trips in the Sierra Nevada Mountains. The summer peacefulness of those mountains had stayed with him. During high school, while he had enthusiastically thrown himself into football, debating, and half a dozen other activities, he had always longed to get away from the city and back into the mountains. When Don had gone to Harvard as a freshman in 1961, one of the first things he had done was to join the mountaineering club. It was through the club, the following year, that I met Don. We liked each other from the start, and soon became best friends. On weekend trips we climbed rock cliffs in New York or ice gullies in New Hampshire. Over Christmas, we spent a week climbing together in Colorado. But while I liked Harvard, Don felt oppressed by the school and decided to drop out the next spring. In March, we regretfully said goodbye to each other at the Boston bus depot. We got together that summer on a Harvard Mountaineering Club expedition to Mount McKinley, when with five others, we made the first direct ascent of its north face.

The next year, Don was back in school. We both lived in Dunster House, and got together to talk mountaineering nearly every day. We climbed again in Colorado during Christmas vacation, this time for eleven days. Meanwhile we planned an expedition to Mount Deborah, in Alaska's Hayes Range, a mountain almost the same height as Huntington and remarkable in many of the same ways. Toward the end of our planning, we decided, perhaps as proof of our friendship, to limit our party to the two of us.

The trip was a failure. We failed to climb Mount Deborah, and ran into a dozen dangerous situations during our forty-two days there. The mountain was made of a crumbly, ugly gray-blue schist, often little solider than the snow plastered to it. The climbing we found on it was spectacular and frightening. Toward the end of the trip, Don fell sixty feet into a crevasse from which it took a whole day to extricate him. On our hike out, we ran out of food. Because of the intensity of being forced together for so long (for more than a month, we never got farther than a rope-length apart), we began to antagonize each other. We spent much of the trip in silent anger and parted at the end of the summer with harsh words. Don had dropped out of Harvard for good, so we saw each other during the next school year not at all. Gradually, though, our feelings of hostility wore off and nostalgia wore on. We wrote each other letters, business-like at first; but we softened, and awkwardly apologized. After that, it didn't take long to decide to give it another try. Don was working in California. The difficulty of arranging another expedition was thus compounded by the difficulty of communication. We independently ran through the possibilities: Foraker, Deborah again, the new south face route on McKinley, Mount Dall, and eventually Huntington. Don and I had glimpsed Huntington among the clouds for a moment in July 1963, as we stood on the top of McKinley. And we had spent long winter afternoons in Washburn's office, before Deborah, going over pictures, some of which had revealed to us the beauty of Huntington. We knew the mountain was likely to be made of the good granite climbers had found nearby, though the French had run into so little rock that they couldn't vouch for its general quality. I went to Washburn's office again, but the verdict we had drawn from the pictures the year before

seemed inflexible: the northwest ridge, to which the
French had beat us, was the only reasonable route.
Huntington is shaped like a triangular pyramid, and
on such a steep mountain only the ridges seem feasible.
But the east ridge, though perhaps not much more difficult than the French route, was bound to be more
hazardous: huge hanging glaciers, the most dangerous
formation imaginable, sprawled obscenely down the
ridge. This route, it was clear, would be the kind that
would put a party in a state of perpetual nervousness.
When the risks depend solely on chance, not skill, the
mountaineer enjoys them as little as anyone. On the
other hand, the south ridge looked incredibly difficult;
it was not so much a ridge as five separate, serrated
peaks, each increasingly higher. To traverse them all
would involve gaining perhaps three times as much
altitude as the east ridge would require, and the necessity of cutting oneself off from the base camp might be
unavoidable.

We thus began to forget about Huntington, not
without a sense of wistful regret—after all, this was
the mountain that had been described as "the most
beautiful in Alaska"; surely it was one of the most
striking in the world. I sat in Washburn's office one
day in January 1965, frustrated by what his pictures
made clear as I flipped through the last of a batch he
had taken only four months before. There were a few
of the west face, a magnificent wall of sheer rock that
Washburn hadn't photographed before, but obviously
impossible . . . unless that barely protruding rib

▲ 23

might divide the avalanches and falling rock . . . but no, it was ridiculous. A pair of pictures, though, made a stereoscopic pair, and by crossing my eyes I could suddenly see the wall in three dimensions. Astonishingly, the rib actually did protrude—what a beautiful, natural line it seemed, then, arrowing straight toward the summit. Full of excitement, I wrote Don that night. Yet as I began to think about it, the hunch seemed more and more impractical. No one had ever climbed a real face in Alaska; nearly all of them are too dangerous. Furthermore, the route looked more difficult than the one we had tried on Deborah, and if we hadn't been able to climb that, how could we hope for Huntington? But I sent copies of the pictures to Don. He quickly wrote back telling me what nonsense the idea was, scolding me and enumerating the problems and disadvantages. Sobered, I agreed and started thinking about Foraker again. But Don's next letter admitted that the Huntington idea had, of course, intrigued him even though it was unthinkable. I wrote back wondering if we could make a reconnaissance over to Huntington at the end of a Foraker expedition. But the fever had traveled 3,000 miles across the antiseptic table of America, and Don's next letter was ungovernably enthusiastic about Huntington. "We've *got* to do it," he almost said. It wasn't hard for me to cast off my newborn doubts and enter with him a pledge to a challenge in which, we admitted to each other, there was certainly less than an even chance of success. Yet a gallant failure, a failure on the sort of route that had never been done in Alaska, seemed more valuable to us than another "good route" in the style of our McKinley climb, one generally admired, but which added little to the possibilities of mountaineering.

2 ▲ The Plan

Don and I agreed that a four-man expedition would be best. Our third, Matt Hale, was a certainty from the beginning. Matt, a year younger than Don and I, had grown up in Virginia, where there was little to stimulate his interest in the mountains. But during summers spent in the Adirondacks of New York, he had discovered the excitement of woods and cliffs, of getting above the trees where there was only sky and rock. Yet he had never been in big mountains, nor hiked any trails west of the Mississippi, before college.

Matt came to Harvard from St. Paul's School in

New Hampshire, where he had done very well academically. But, like Don, Matt probably felt more of an inclination toward the athletic than toward the scholarly life. He joined the mountaineering club at the beginning of his freshman year. Matt's father had also been a member of the HMC, during the years that Washburn and Bates had been there. Perhaps Matt was conscious of family tradition; in any case, he soon discovered that mountaineering would be his primary interest in school.

I first met Matt on a beginners' trip to the Shawangunk Cliffs in New York, in the fall of 1962. While all the other beginners were sweating and trembling on the easiest routes (as a beginner should, we presumed, if he had a safe respect for the mountains), Matt was having astonishingly little trouble. He surprised me at first. He looked thin and frail, and he was almost painfully shy, speaking politely and only when someone asked him a question. He was climbing so well, however, that he was attracting a lot of attention among the older members of the club. Matt seemed almost oblivious to the attention. Obviously, he was not showing off. I liked this quality in him immediately.

However, prodigies often appear in a sport like climbing, especially in rock climbing. Balance, strength, and smoothness may be as much innate as learned; hence a beginner often can climb a very difficult cliff, with a rope from above. It is the subtle matter of judgment that makes a good mountaineer, that requires season after season in the mountains; the HMC's (or any other club's) function, far more than to teach skills, is to teach judgment. Often, the rock-climbing prodigy loses interest as the novelty wears off, and as he sees how much there is yet to learn, even for him. Matt seemed to be the opposite sort. He wanted to know everything about climbing, and he was clearly aware of the gaps in his experience. He seemed as much embarrassed by the attention he was arousing as eager for it. His shyness, of course, could have camouflaged a strong private ambition, but so could the enthusiasm of any of us.

Matt climbed with Don and me in Colorado over Christmas, 1963. During the school year, he quickly became an accomplished climber in all respects. After Deborah, I climbed with Matt in Colorado in August, where we first tackled a high mountain together. We began to sense a technical co-operation that is rare even between long-standing partners. With Don gone from Harvard my senior year, Matt became my best friend.

We had talked about the expedition as early as December 1964. Matt was attracted to Huntington, but admitted he had little basis on which to judge our chances. He seemed wary of our wild enthusiasm, especially in the face of a doubtful success. It took longer to infect him with the excitement of the plan, with what Don and I called "commitment."

We needed a fourth. Matt and I climbed together often during the school year, discussing possibilities, keeping our eyes open for the "right" man. I enjoyed climbing with Matt then more than with anyone else. We had developed the camaraderie and communicative precision that makes a good "rope." We were roughly equal in ability, and got increasingly better at much the same rate, so that our climbing partnership never grew one-sided. I tried to share with Matt some of the anticipatory pleasure I felt for Alaska, an exultation blended of nostalgia and the appeal of a "perfect" route, untempered by fear or reluctance. But he couldn't help but feel divided, as I had felt before my first expedition, between irrational fear and rational conservatism, between the dregs of dread and the appeal of the plan. His imagination dwelt on reports he had heard of post-expedition exhaustion and satiation, projecting over two months the little discomforts he had known camping and climbing on weekends. (How long could he stand eating the same dehydrated foods, drinking melted snow, never having his hands warm outside a sleeping bag, never being able to relax in front of a warm fire?) He had no nostalgia to feed his excitement, no experience to cement his expectations. He knew that big mountains are always dangerous.

This is to say that Matt, as yet, lacked the feeling of total commitment that Don and I not only had but demanded. Yet one might well wonder why we should ask that kind of involvement—indeed, how was it possible for us to feel it? Without being necessarily "antisocial," climbing of the sort we were preparing for, a four-man party alone for two months in the most rugged mountains in North America, requires if not a fundamental loneliness of soul, at least a temporary ability to do without most of the other people in the world. Don and I had found we could enjoy long periods of self-sufficiency in the mountains. If we grew to miss many of civilization's comforts, their appeal never equaled the taut excitement of the way of life we could lead on expeditions. Although I could rationalize it, I never understood the intensity of my feeling for Alaska. To chalk it up to nostalgia would have avoided the question. To observe that once life has become momentarily precious it can never again fail to dissatisfy when it is merely routine still barely gets beneath the skin of the problem. The sense of commitment was, for us, not primarily a personal loyalty we felt toward each other. The expedition's personnel were interchangeable in a way its ambition was not; that is, for me not to have climbed with Don would have been disappointing, but not to have climbed at all would have been much more so. Hence the mountains, in a sense, could mean more to me than people could. But what sort of relationship is possible between a man and a mountain? If any, an obviously one-sided one; and if the mountain only mirrors the man, if the route he chooses is not made out of rock, snow, and ice so much as out of some tortured translation of his ego, then that clean love he can feel toward his objective would become a barren narcissism. "Have we vanquished an enemy?" Mallory said. "None but ourselves." Put that way, it sounds noble, it rings with aphoristic authority. But what would happen, I wonder,

if the self could be vanquished? What would be left of
life but to live it out in smug lethargy? Could any man
who had vanquished himself ever want to climb another
mountain? I would like to believe that Mallory himself
could never have relaxed into complacency; that when
he climbed into the clouds on Everest never to be seen
again, he died, like Terray, still full of dreams of other
summits. I need to believe, if only to explain climbing,
that the dissatisfactions of life ultimately become its
joys, that to resolve may be only to die, not to answer.
Therefore for me the mountain must be there, real; it
must, as much as anything I will ever have contact or
combat with, exist outside myself. The mind may be
wonderful, and even self-sufficient, but for the mountaineer it is not large enough by itself. It and the heart
and the body, all that make up man, require response,
not only love and co-operation but hindrance and hate,
not only friends but enemies. If a mountain, Huntington for instance, was not an enemy we could impute
any malice to, did that make it a less formidable one?
What can be more appalling than the sovereign power
of nature directed by no mind, spirited by no will, indifferent, dwarfing? What vision of malignity can equal
the darkness of that of a universe that is running down,
of a cosmos that neither orders nor obeys man's yearn-
ings, but blindly collapses toward a final motionlessness?
Death, our only glimpse of that entropic end, has its
seductive fascination. Hence, the risks of climbing stir
and motivate us, just as other risks may someday stir
some cosmic voyager.

But I suppose this does not really explain. At best it can hint at what the mountain meant to me; yet if I understood that at all well I would explain it better. If I understood it, though, perhaps I wouldn't care enough about it to want to explain it. Nor does all this explain how Don felt, or how Matt eventually would. The mountain was beautiful; perhaps that is all that need be said. That, and that it would be very hard to climb.

But as the months flew past, and Matt and I in Cambridge and Don in San Francisco went through the welcome frenzy of figuring out every detail of food, time, and equipment, we still lacked a fourth. At last we agreed to ask an Alaskan mountaineer whom Don and I had met on McKinley. He wrote, regretting that he'd be unavailable for the summer. The same obstacle snagged our second choice, a Washington native who had made Mount Foraker's second ascent.

Lurking in the back of my mind had been another possibility: a close friend of ours at Harvard, a climber whose only drawback seemed to be inexperience. But Ed Bernd had learned climbing more quickly in his two years with the HMC than anyone I'd ever known. In addition, that spring he seemed to get even better, as if he had skipped several grades to emerge as a good technical climber. That kind of progress always makes one wary, but Matt and I agreed that Ed showed uncommon judgment as well. Personally, he would be very good. His outstanding characteristic was a cheerful easygoingness that Matt, Don, and I were incapable of.

In the middle of April Matt and I went up to talk to Ed. When we asked him to go with us, he didn't know at first what to say. He was too flattered to conceal it, but we insisted that he not let that influence his decision. Whether or not it did, only he could have said. Yet there never seemed, after the first moment, to be any hesitation in his mind. Even though it would be hard for him to finance, he assured us he would make it work. Ed was like that. If he wanted things to work, they usually did. He immediately joined us for the final planning period, a last six weeks of school that passed beyond the hectic into the frantic. Not only did Ed's buoyancy through it all surprise and please us, but it added to our confidence. Don noticed in our letters how perfectly the expedition had congealed. Now that Ed was with us it seemed ridiculous that we should ever have had doubts about him.

So despite finals, despite running the HMC, putting out its biennial journal, and helping to arrange another expedition, Matt, Ed, and I spent three or four hours a day preparing for Huntington. We would get together at dinner in Quincy House, so as not to waste the time merely eating that we could use for talking. The discussions would start rigorously: how many angle pitons we were going to take *had* to be decided today; could we talk that guy out of his microbus for less than $800? What was Ed going to do for a down jacket? By the third dessert we were always lost in aimless speculation: Ed's "What if" trailed into Matt's "The chances are"—both drowned out by my "Last year on Deborah"—. Don's letters grew more and more excited and less and less coherent. It was becoming obvious that the time it took for him to write them (since our poverty precluded cross-country phone calls) was actually beginning to interfere with more important things. There just didn't seem to be any time left. Yet had it taken any longer for summer to come we couldn't have waited.

Everything around me, the color of the sunset over the Charles, the shape of Leverett Towers, took on the aura of an invisible world of pure rock, ice, and air 5,000 miles away. When I descended the steps in Harvard Square to the MTA train I half expected to find in the dark the cold blue inside of a crevasse. When I scanned clusters of symbols in a detested math book, I saw a joyous jumble of rock towers strung along some windswept ridge.

Whether or not Ed and Matt suffered the same hallucinations, the obstacles and hours proved finite. One afternoon in early June, after a ritual beer at Cronin's (the precedent having been set by Don and me the year before), we lumbered west in the overloaded microbus we had bought for $800 anyway, intending to meet Don at my home in Boulder, Colorado, for a last fit of packing before we could head for Alaska.

We made only one stop so Ed could drop some things off at his home near Philadelphia. Ed had lived there all his life. He had grown up in typically urban surroundings. Family vacations had ranged as far as Jones Beach, but there was nothing in his childhood to spur an interest in mountains. He had read about mountains, seen hills, but the high, white cold of Alaska might have seemed remote and uninteresting to him then. Yet Ed seemed to succeed at everything he tried. He was a school hero: tall, and ruggedly handsome, he became a football star, president of his high-school class three years in a row, the most popular student, and the first from his school ever to go to Harvard: at eighteen, almost something of a civic monument. At Harvard, the HMC had been for Ed just another activity at first, something new to try. But as he discovered the fear and fascination of climbing, he must have realized that this was an entirely different sort of thing. Mountains might end in summits, but there was no limit to the mountaineer's urge. In the summer after his freshman year, he hitch-hiked to Canada. There, for the first time, he saw the Rockies. They looked huge and mysterious. Sadly enough, Ed couldn't find anybody to go climbing with him, so he had to content himself with a few hikes among their lower reaches. By the time he got back, the mountains had infected him. The bigger, the better; if he could have gone to Alaska alone, he probably would have, much as his parents might have opposed it.

We arrived at his house at 3:00 A.M., waking up Ed's parents, whom Matt and I met then for the first time. They were glad we had stopped, even at that hour. Ed's mother made us sandwiches while we talked. We sensed the edge of an awkward feeling, because none of us really wanted to talk about Huntington, yet that was clearly all any of us could think about. Then we got ready to leave; they told us to be careful. We said goodbye, stepping out the door into the cool, wet scent of azaleas that saturated the predawn air.

3 ▲ The Long Road

Don met us in Boulder. It had been nearly a year since
I'd seen him, and I scarcely recognized him now. He
had a magnificent tan, a mustache, and was thirty
pounds lighter than I'd ever known him, in the best
shape of his life. Ed, who hadn't got to know Don
very well in their one year together at Harvard, quickly
grew to like him now. The pace of preparation, decel-
erated briefly during our drive to Colorado, picked up
again. To divide and pack the food we usurped most
of two houses for a week. A further complication was
our having to buy all our supplies in Denver, and on

our second day there, the worst flood in the city's history hit it. We bought our canned food the afternoon before the warehouse they came from burned down in the night; we had to outwit National Guardsmen to get across town, and by the time we were ready to leave, the only roads open led, fortunately, to the north.

Everything we would need on the mountain somehow managed to fit into the microbus, even leaving room for us to be comfortable. The back of the bus became our bedroom where two people could lie full-length in sleeping bags. We were determined to drive straight through to Alaska, a feat that didn't seem difficult with four drivers. The year before, Don and I had driven nonstop from Boston, six days and six nights that passed in a delirium of No-Doz numbness, oncoming headlights, and trees that suddenly jumped into the road. But this year the road was shorter, because of our Colorado headstart, and the driver, far from ever having to feel ill-rested, could be reasonably sure of someone to talk to during his spell at the wheel. Near the Wyoming border we stretched the expedition budget to include the latest *Playboy* and a bagful of firecrackers, the latter of which somehow showed up in Ed's pockets on the Tokositna Glacier on July 4.

The driving, for a while, was easy. As we got farther and farther north, the land grew rockier and less populated, the air cleaner and colder, the nights shorter. At stops for gas or picnic supplies, we played football on the highway, or, if a building looked challenging enough, worked out first ascent routes on its walls. After a few moments of frantic exercise, we would pile back into the bus, to lie catching our breath as the driver headed north again. We had planned to stop to eat, but we found it easy to spread our picnics in the back of the bus.

Ed especially enjoyed the driving. He waited eagerly for his turn, and never seemed to have any trouble staying alert, even in the small hours of the night. In fact, when someone else was driving, Ed would stay awake as long as he could, staring out the window at everything that flew past, even during the long stretches that were monotonously similar. Ed had been through some of this country the year before, hitch-hiking, but he could never see enough of it. Don and I were familiar with it, too, but less curious. Don, who probably had been working at a more feverish pitch than any of us during the last month, used the trip to relax, sleeping as often as he could. But he had trouble getting a good sleep in the moving bus, as did Matt. Sometimes one or the other of them would dream the bus was going off the road, and wake with a lurch to grab the wheel. Ed, who always seemed to be driving during the night, had no trouble fighting them off.

All in all, though, it was a relaxed and relaxing trip. Wyoming meandered by, and a long night's drive into Montana got us to Billings just as we ran out of gas. During these days, the first all four of us had shared, we began to feel a cohesive spirit, to believe that we were an expedition. Just as we would later on a high glacier and a precipitous wall of rock, we carried with us everything we needed, and cared about little except getting to our goal.

We had decided to cross Glacier National Park, not only to whet our mountain appetites, but because its border station stayed open most of the night. As it was, we got there in broad daylight. Poverty-stricken as we were becoming, we could scarcely justify to ourselves spending the half-dollar-a-head entrance fee; so Matt and I hid under the sleeping bags, several boxes of food, and the distractingly opened *Playboy* a few miles before the entrance. It was terriby hot under all that stuff. When the bus came to a stop we held our breath. We could hear Don's end of a conversation; then we were moving again. I started to fight my way out, but Ed put his hand on top of the bag and whispered tensely, "Stay under there! There's a detour and the gate's only three miles ahead."

There was no choice but to suffocate a little longer. Enough time seemed to go by for anything but a donkey to travel three miles, but still no gate. Ed whispered, "Don't move now."

We held our breath again. The bus stopped. We heard the jingle of change as Don paid the attendant.

"Yeah. Just two of us."

A deadly pause. Then Ed's nervous voice:

"No, that's nothing but boxes and sleeping bags and stuff."

I tried to make my heart beat a little more gently so it wouldn't shake the bus. Then Ed yelled, "Move out of here, Don!"

The bus shot off with a squeal of rubber. Matt and I were flung back and forth among the boxes as the bus negotiated some sharp turns.

"Oh God," screamed Ed, "they're coming after us!"

I tried to burrow deeper in with the food. Would they shoot first and ask questions later? Would we have to run a roadblock at the exit?

Suddenly Ed started laughing hysterically. He'd gone berserk. Then Don started laughing, too, and the bus slowed to a stop. Matt and I peeked out from our sarcophagus. We were parked beside a peaceful lake, obviously far inside the park. And Don and Ed couldn't stop laughing.

It took Matt and me a while to regain enough composure to compliment their performance. Then we had lunch, congratulating ourselves on saving a dollar.

But crime does not pay. A few hundred yards beyond our lunch spot, the engine suddenly howled like a cat caught in a garbage disposal; we limped to a pull-out, where it died. The nearest Volkswagen dealer, the park ranger informed us, was in Kalispell, forty miles back, and there was a man who, for a dollar a mile, would be more than glad to tow us there. Necessity is the daughter of disaster, so we accepted the offer.

When we got to Kalispell, it seemed to be Sunday. The tow truck left our bus in the parking lot of the VW place, where we would have to wait for morning.

At the time Mount Huntington might as well have been on the dark side of the moon. We felt miserable. Even football offered us little solace. With nothing to do we walked down the long, dusty road into the main part of town. Outside an open supermarket we held a colloquium to determine whether a hunk of cheese or a loaf of bread would offer the better combination of fillingness and nutrition for the money. Finally we skipped both. After this demonstration of our will to economize, we walked a little farther and decided to waste a dollar each on a movie.

Gradually our spirits improved. We held a conference to decide whose parents we dared call for money, and scraped together all we could of our own. Out of Don's and my pockets came traveler's checks; Matt dug for some loose bills; and Ed dipped into the emergency cache he had sewn into his underpants. The very sacrifices we made healed our feelings; soon we were joking again, and we slept well that night on the parking lot. The next morning, a man put a new engine in our bus for a hundred dollars less than we had anticipated. Joyously we set out again around noon. Though disclaiming any superstitiousness, all four of us paid for readmittance to the park. Without even crossing our fingers, we passed the spot of our earlier demise. But a few miles farther, Don swerved to avoid a tourist troupe blundering down the middle of the road, and hit some rocks that inflicted simultaneous blowouts on our right front and rear tires.

This time only Matt and Don had to leave the park, and they courageously found service stations before Kalispell. They returned, the bus rolled again, and at last we crossed the mountains into Canada determined to push or carry the bus the rest of the way if it quit on us again.

We got through Calgary with comparative ease and stopped for final purchases in Edmonton, the last big city on our route and the farthest outpost of the land of reasonable prices. At last, about two weeks behind schedule, we began the 1,200-mile trek of the Alaska Highway, nearly all of it dirt road. Every gas station along the way pumped nostalgia into Don and me for the two previous years we had traveled the road. We stopped at Liard Hot Springs near the Yukon border and bathed in the steaming pools in the rain. We talked to a man who had driven alone from South Carolina and had just decided to go back because it was getting too cold. But to us, the cold spoke only of the nearness of our mountain, as did the suddenly lengthening days. Driving became a pleasure now; the thirty miles an hour the road demanded permitted us to see what we were passing.

Yet it was all the same, a wall of scraggly trees that reached from one end of the Yukon to the other. Their monotony echoed a loneliness not so much primeval as insidious, empty. I was physically aware that back of the first trees on the right-hand side stretched a dull gloom unbroken to the Arctic coast, far beyond the distant MacKenzie River; that, on the other side, the forests subtly inclined until, abruptly, the trees confronted the frozen edge of the St. Elias Range. I was dimly aware that nothing touched that gloom but three months of rain and nine of snow; that rivers raged somewhere in that wilderness where only bears and birds had ever heard them. The road is not beautiful. Its scenery oppresses rather than enthralls. Wordsworth could not have written there. One senses in that country only a self-sufficient, ragged evenness, broken occasionally by the whelming power of a river in flood.

In the afternoon we approached the St. Elias Range, and glimpsed through the foothills one of the high peaks far within it, perhaps Mount Kennedy. The wind blew us around Kluane Lake; soon we were driving in a furious storm. The gusts lashed our bus with a staccato of rain through an unnatural, foreboding darkness as we crossed the swollen Donjek, the river along which Washburn and Bates had had to backtrack twenty miles to find a crossing in 1937, during their escape from Lucania. But overnight the storm blew itself out. I woke around 4:00 A.M. to find the bus stopped in the road in a heavy drizzle several miles short of Alaska. Our vehicle seemed to respect national boundaries too highly. We couldn't figure out what was wrong, and it was no fun lying under the bus in the cold mud guessing. At last two natural mechanics who happened by unplugged our fuel line with a coat-hanger.

Suddenly we were in Alaska. Matt didn't acknowledge my boisterous claim that things immediately looked bigger and better. Instead he replied that all he noticed were more trees and more holes in the road, now that it was paved. We stopped for a picnic and shave near the Delta River, then started down the highway to Anchorage. Along the road we could see a different

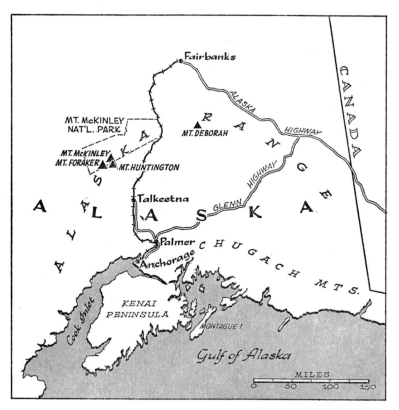

South-Central Alaska

kind of mountain, almost Colorado-like; but, as if to assure us we hadn't driven in a circle, the huge, clean Matanuska Glacier sprawled out of the Chugach Range almost down to the road. We spent a day in Anchorage gathering the last of our equipment, a few impulsively chosen delicacies for our candlelight dinners in August, and the indispensable pint of victory brandy. Then we gassed up the bus, prayed over it, and started our last drive through the night to the tiny town of Talkeetna.

I was driving at 3:00 A.M., the others asleep, as the bus topped a little ridge suddenly to reveal the Alaska Range filling the horizon. There was a cloud layer at about 12,000 feet, so the summits of McKinley and Foraker and a few others seemed cut off; but the recognizable bulks beneath, eighty miles away, through the occasional gap in which rays of the northern sun flashed, seemed to draw the bus onward the last few miles to Talkeetna. We arrived, threw our sleeping bags down on Don Sheldon's airstrip, and waited for morning, when we would accost Alaska's most famous bush pilot.

4 ▲ The Unknown Glacier

Sheldon was glad to see us, but the clouds had lowered around McKinley by morning, so that he couldn't fly us in right away. We unloaded the bus in his hangar while he showed us relics from other expeditions stored there. There was an especially large pile from the French Huntington expedition to which Sheldon urged us to help ourselves. Within a few hours we were ready to go, but the weather was getting worse. There was nothing to do but wait. We managed a few patchy conversations with Sheldon, who literally never stood still. We wanted to make sure he could land in the

ALLEY

LOWER PARK

STEGOSAUR

PITCH 20

PITCH 10

J. LEINUNG

ROUTE ON WEST FACE
OF MT. HUNTINGTON

o Belay points · o—o Pitches

◇ Camps ✝ Site of accident

To identify this segment with the entire west face of the mountain, see Photo Number 2 in picture section.

For further details of the specific stages of the ascent and descent, see Appendices, pages 149-153.

First 5½ pitches are not shown.

narrow basin of the upper Tokositna Glacier; he impatiently said, "Yep, we'll get her fixed up," and forged back into the middle of whatever anecdote he had been telling. His wife, Roberta, smiled at us knowingly, then tried to interpret her husband's cryptic assurances to us when he was gone.

We wasted as much time as we could writing letters, walking around Talkeetna, or greeting the twice-daily train. Matt and I, tired of football, found an old softball and bat in the schoolhouse, repaired the backstop behind it, and invented an elaborate two-man game. A couple of eight-year-old girls fell in love with the newly arrived diamond heroes; in despair we converted them to outfielders. With them they brought a retinue of more fearless, younger natives, who insisted on digging holes and tunnels in the sand between the pitcher's mound and first base. Most of the time our game was reduced to a bunting contest.

Don, who was at last in his element, spent the hours fiddling with equipment, studying the maps, or climbing on top of Sheldon's hangar to look at the weather. Ed, on the other hand, seemed gloomier than usual. He sat in the bus, writing long letters, and declined our invitations to softball or football. He seemed apprehensive. Perhaps it was a combination of excitement and awe. We walked a few blocks down the small lane that was Talkeetna's main street, to the edge of the Susitna River. The churning current, nearly a mile wide, was carrying dead trees and branches swiftly past us. Fascinated, we stared for most of an hour at the intricate weavings of the river. For me, it was like a glimpse of the mountains themselves: the mountains which, however motionless, had the same kind of chaotic power.

By evening of the second day, the clouds lifted from the range. Sheldon told us to be ready at four the next morning, so that he could fly us in with the best possible snow conditions for landing. As we went to sleep, I still pessimistically expected it to be raining in the morning. But Sheldon woke us with, "Let's get a move on, she's a fine one." Matt and I quickly dressed, dumped our gear in Sheldon's Cessna, and put on our down jackets, despite the 70-degree warmth of Talkeetna, for we would step out of the plane in a cold glacial corridor at 9,000 feet. Just before taking off, Sheldon seemed to remember something. He got out his jackknife and started to prune one of the trees in his yard. Matt and I were impatient to go. I started to ask Sheldon if that couldn't wait till after he'd flown us in. Then I realized that he wanted some boughs to throw out of the plane while he was over the glacier, in order to judge the shape of its slope, which would be otherwise unreadable in the flat light of mid-morning. Matt piled the boughs on his lap, Sheldon started the engine, and we sputtered down the rocky runway.

Just before it seemed we would plunge into the Susitna River, at about forty-five miles an hour, we floundered into the air. The plane was probably overloaded, but once in the air it seemed content. So were Matt and I. Eighty miles away, the Alaska Range stuck into the faultless sky, differentiable only as three white masses: McKinley, Hunter, and Foraker. There was nothing else on which to fix our attention for the first fifteen minutes except the trackless tundra beneath us, threaded by silver rivers that wound their ways outward, like snakes escaping the mountains that spawned them. After a while we could pick out Huntington, its summit visible above a thin cloud layer. Its separation from the mountains near it seemed to increase. Then, as we passed over the snout of the glacier, Huntington was suddenly silhouetted against the sky rather than against McKinley. Its astonishing sharpness struck us, even though we were prepared for it. Suddenly the clouds broke; we were right in the gorge of the Tokositna. In a matter of seconds we flashed past the west face. Both of us had just run out of film. But we stared at the wall, so close I was half afraid the plane would crash. Sheldon banked sharply left, heading us up the basin toward Hunter. I looked at our pilot's face. He didn't seem perturbed, yet these incredible walls were just outside the plane's window. We were obviously too high to land, but too low to clear the pass ahead. The plane banked suddenly and as I gave up hope, Sheldon made a complete circle within the basin, lowering as he turned. Then he instructed us to throw the boughs out, carefully, one at a time. As they whipped out of my grasp, Sheldon kept circling, watching each one fall. The light on the glacier was so flat that the boughs never seemed to hit it, but simply to stop falling. We spiraled lower and lower. Then Sheldon said, "OK.

We're taking her in." He made a last turn and straightened out. I still couldn't tell where the snow was, whether it was fifty feet below or five hundred. Suddenly a wall of whiteness seemed to leap in front of the plane. Sheldon pulled back on the stick; the stall warning screamed; we topped the rise and landed in one motion. I kept saying "beautiful, beautiful" but Sheldon told us to hurry up and get the stuff out of the plane. I opened the door and jumped out; the snow was crisp and solid. Matt threw our stuff out; then we stood clear, and Sheldon took off down the glacier to get Ed and Don. We saw him round the bend, a dot now against the surrounding walls. Then even the sound of the engine was gone, and we stood there alone.

All there was for us to do was to place the boughs in a row to indicate a runway for Sheldon's next landing. We put on our snowshoes, roped up, and got this done quickly. Then we sat on our packs and waited. It wasn't nearly as cold as I had anticipated; in fact the fierce sun made the glacier seem like a summer beach. We were far up its northwest branch, much closer to Hunter than to Huntington. Steep avalanche slopes walled this precipitous basin. At the other end of it, five miles away, was our west face. It was too bad Sheldon hadn't been able to land closer, for it would probably take us most of a week to get our supplies over to a base camp; but that he had been able to land at all seemed remarkable.

In 1906 Belmore Browne's party had crossed the mouth of the Tokositna, putting a camp near a huge boulder that marked the middle of it. But for them, no one had ever stood on the glacier until this day, June 29, 1965. No one had ever explored any of its nine branches, which wind back into mazes of unclimbed, unnamed peaks, even though several parties have walked the full lengths of the neighboring glaciers, the Ruth and the Kahiltna. Our original plan had been to hike in; but the delays that had put us two weeks behind schedule demanded the quickest possible approach. Still, as I sat on this new glacier, enjoying all the sensual novelty of the air, the stillness, and the sun, I had a feeling that we had cheated, or at least a regret that we had forfeited the experiences of hiking seventy miles across the tundra and up the glacier. After two expeditions on which we had walked both in and out, flying, for Don and me, had to be a mixed pleasure.

Of course Matt's thoughts at the moment were different. He seemed, understandably, subdued; to suddenly find oneself in a place like this for the first time was bound to be chastening. Matt probably felt neither the sense of having cheated nor the sense of having missed anything. But I couldn't really know what he was thinking; and I wanted to, then. I could remember my first sight of McKinley, but that was from a road. I could try to empathize with him, but he was difficult to interpret. He couldn't explain the strange mixture of sensations he must have felt then, even if he had wanted to; and perhaps he didn't.

But what I write now must in some way stand for all four of us. Climbing together, which forces men close to each other physically and sometimes spiritually, still can't overcome the irreducible barriers of their separate selves. Nor can writing ultimately translate the experience. So in words, all that may ultimately get through is some third-hand filtration of life that was once lived. A man's best moments seem to go by before he notices them; and he spends a large part of his life reaching back for them, like a runner for a baton that will never come. In disappointment, he grows nostalgic; and nostalgia inevitably blurs the memory of the immediate thrill, which, simply because it had to be instantaneous, could not have lasted. Now that our whole expedition has passed, now that I sit in a warm room with a pencil and blank paper before me, instead of rock and snow, I feel our vanished moments forever lost. I want to wreathe their remnants with feelings I never felt before, especially not while the moments lived. The frustration of it reminds me, too, how I felt sitting on my pack on June 29 waiting for the plane, wanting to know what Matt was thinking. People placed in any isolation, even together, lose something of their humanity; and a style of isolation so complete as mountaineering begs for someone to understand it, to convey it as it is, not as the melodrama of death and blind courage it seems to resemble. Courage plays a smaller part than the tension and dependence that being alone together in a dangerous place forces on men. The drama is a largely internal one, whose conflict stems from the stress between private desire and co-operative skill that climbing imposes. Perhaps this is why mountaineers are usually inarticulate; everything having to do with climbing seems to stifle the soul's urge to communicate. Part of the strange sorrow I felt then, on the glacier, must have arisen from the dilemma no more peculiar to me than to anyone, of being born alone with the desire not to be. If the mind can escape itself little better than the body can, still, something goes on between men, even in mountains, something lost in the static rigor of reporting it. The men who have gone through the tension of an expedition have not written about it well. No one has explained the basic truths of climbing, the interplay beneath its alternating fear and hope. What goes on in those lonely places is so much more than pitons hammered, camps moved; what goes on, not only within men, but between them, is sometimes profound. Yet I feel that I cannot get at the heart of it either. Perhaps I care too much; perhaps so long as I care, I can never explain; perhaps if I stop caring, I will forget.

Nor did these thoughts go through my head then. There was too much to see; it was only a slight pang, a feeling rather than a thought. There were little things to do, like putting glacier cream on our faces, or reading the temperature. Then suddenly we heard the plane's buzz, and Sheldon flew into sight around the bend in the glacier. He landed perfectly. Ed stepped out of the plane with a raucous whoop and pulled a remarkable pile of rope and food boxes out of the plane. In a few moments, Sheldon was off again. With

Ed, we moved our supplies nearer the center of the glacier, in case the avalanches had unusually long run-outs. Before we expected it, Sheldon was back with Don and the last of our equipment. It was starting to cloud up, so Sheldon was anxious to get on his way. He snapped a few pictures of the four of us beside the plane, with our cameras, and took off.

We tried to think what we might possibly have forgotten. We had enough salt, plenty of matches; I'd even brought the football. Then someone remembered the radio. It was still in Sheldon's hangar. Matt and Ed were a little disturbed but Don and I tried to cajole them out of worrying. We hadn't had a radio on Mc-Kinley; the one we took to Deborah had quit working after a week, and we had to carry its six useless pounds all the rest of the trip. At best, a radio is a big help in an emergency; at worst, a false source of confidence. We could do without it. I think Don and I even partly welcomed the further isolation imposed by its absence.

After pitching our tents, we basked in the sun the rest of the day, not out of laziness, but because one travels on Alaskan glaciers at night. Until late July, it is light enough even at midnight for comfortable travel. Until then one never needs a flashlight or a candle, even for reading inside the tent. We fell asleep in the afternoon, then set out at 2:00 A.M. with heavy loads. The four of us were roped together at 150-foot intervals so that we would always be stretched as far apart as possible in case of a crevasse fall. I led; Matt came second, Ed third, and Don brought up the rear.

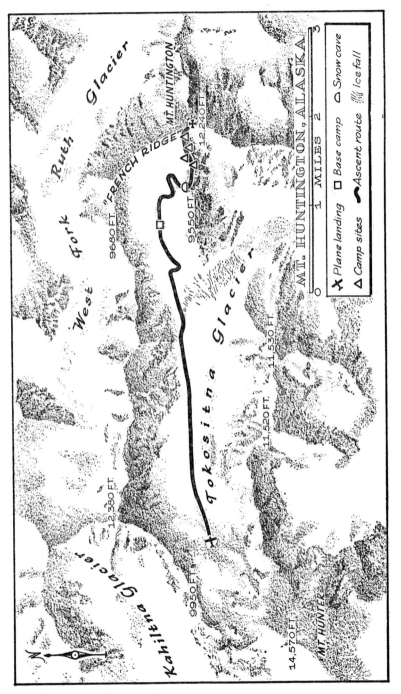

Mt. Huntington and the Tokositna Glacier

The Tokositna was, for Matt and Ed, their first glacier; for Don and me, our first since the day a year
before when Don had plunged into a crevasse on the
Susitna Glacier, badly cutting his face in the second of
two serious crevasse falls in as many days. Now the
glacial surface seemed utterly featureless under a
gloomy, overcast sky. I felt nervous leading, especially
since the temperature was a warm 35° F., but the
snow's crust stayed firm all night.

Crevasses, just as they are popularly imagined, are
long gaping seams in the surface of the ice, formed by
the terrible strain of a glacier's flow. The deepest of
them drop several hundred feet. But the open holes
are no threat, except to the mountaineer's patience
in skirting those that are too wide to step or jump
across. What the climber fears, with the brutish terror
reserved for only a few phenomena, like avalanches
and falling rocks, are the hidden crevasses, the ones
that form delicate skins of snow-bridge only a foot or
two thick and which blend treacherously into the general contours of the glacier. Traveling on the Gillam
Glacier in 1964, Don had fallen sixty feet into one of
these hidden crevasses, with a 70-pound pack on his
back. It was a miracle that he hadn't been seriously
hurt. Even so, it took a full, lonely day for the two
of us, barely able to hear each other's shouts at the
tops of our voices, to improvise a way to get him out.
Then, the very next day, when our problems at last
seemed to be over, he had fallen thirty feet into another crevasse, sustaining cuts that had infected badly

by the time we were able to get out to civilization five days later. The mountaineer never walks easily on a big, unknown glacier. Although he can read all sorts of subtle signs to try to outguess them, crevasses remain one of the least predictable of mountain hazards. And they are often extremely difficult to get out of, even for the uninjured climber, because they characteristically bulge halfway down, leaving overhanging walls of ice above, ready to collapse inward at the slightest pressure. Had I not been safely outside with a rope, Don could never have escaped the first crevasse he fell into the year before. Those icy sepulchers are dark, wet places; corridors shoot in all directions, hideously honeycombing the glacier; and shelves of ice that seem to bottom the crevasses often thinly mask even deeper chambers. In the early days of climbing in the Alps, when ladies in full-length dresses and petticoats strolled the ice, accompanied by well-dressed men who carried shepherd's crooks instead of ice axes, far more deaths were caused by crevasse falls than by any other kind of accident. The gothic imagination, moreover, was stirred to a morbid spasm by the occasional appearance, years later, of well-preserved parts of recognizable bodies, disgorged from the mouths of the ever flowing glaciers. No wonder, then, that contemporary artists painted these crevasses not as holes in the surrounding glacier so much as bottomless gulfs which, themselves, surrounded icy islands of safety.

But the Tokositna seemed pretty safe, at least with the snow as firm as we found it. We went slowly and carefully, and I never stuck so much as a foot in a crevasse. The first three miles of our hike were downhill; then we negotiated a level stretch, the worst-crevassed area yet, before climbing a mile up the other branch of the basin, the one that lay beneath Huntington. Along this route we passed under the uniformly impressive walls of a number of unnamed peaks. For diversion we picked out "impossible" routes that climbers fifty years from now might try, impossible not because of steepness or length or innate difficulty, but because they were swept by avalanches, or because great ice blocks broke off and hurtled down them.

In five and a half hours we had reached the spot beneath our face that we decided to call base camp. Wearily we dumped our loads—it seemed such a pitiful pile for all that work—and contemplated the face as we ate lunch. The temperature was rising and a drizzly snow-rain began to fall. We turned around and hiked back to camp, the long, final uphill stretch particularly tiring us. Our new base camp was actually at a lower altitude than where the plane had landed.

We got a late start the next night, because our tired backs encouraged us to improvise a sled. We taped together sixteen food boxes, about twice what we could have carried, then set up a complicated harness for pulling the thing. But we had to plow away a layer of fresh snow, and the hauling was more work than it was worth. The sled fell apart after two miles, so we simply carried half our load the rest of the way over. Especially tired that night, we slept until 5:30 A.M., and the next day would have been wasted if the snow conditions hadn't stayed so remarkably good. By 9:30 A.M. the temperature was 42° F., yet the snow surface remained hard and safe. In two more days, we had everything we needed at base camp. Already we were making better time on the glacier as we started to get in good shape. We finished the drudgery of hauling on July 4, a beautiful day; Ed appropriately set off a bunch of his loudest firecrackers to celebrate. The echoes rang all over the basin. Since it was so warm anyway, the rest of us refused to attribute any of the countless avalanches on the surrounding walls to Ed's noises.

For several days in a row, Ed and Matt occupied one of our two-man tents, while Don and I slept in the other. We pitched them so that we could roll the sleeve doors together, making a nice "hotel" arrangement, especially handy not only for cooking, but also for conversation. Both Matt and Ed had seemed a bit depressed during the first days; certainly Ed was less buoyant than usual, and Matt acted unenthusiastic. Neither Don nor I worried about this. It was an inevitable reaction to the sudden transition from the outside world; to five days spent in the dwarfing presence of bigger mountains than they had ever seen, the most awesome of which they would soon try to climb; to five days of nocturnal trudging across a glacier featureless enough to lull the mind into boredom, yet always dangerous; to five days filled with the nameless anxieties awakened by a route we could see but not yet attack. But Matt and Ed did their share of the work; if they

left most of the decision-making to us, they were cheerful enough about going along with them. And Ed's
firecracker outburst suggested that presence would
make his heart grow fonder, as it would also for Matt
and Don and me.

What I appreciated most was the absence of the
tension Don and I had felt last year from the very
beginning. On Deborah, because there were only two
of us, we went through hours of waiting out storms
in the tent, refusing to speak to each other, wishing we
could see someone else, anyone else, yet unable to get
away from each other. If those worst moments had
been balanced by periods of intense companionship,
there still had never been a time after the first few
days when we could totally relax. We got to know
each other, in superficial ways, better than people
should; in some important ways, not well enough.

There were recesses in Don, whole areas masked by
his outward calm, his self-sufficiency in the mountains,
that I couldn't explore. I suppose he felt the same way
about me. Once or twice he had said he couldn't understand how I could get so suddenly angry for no apparent reason. On Deborah we had had to hold some
part of ourselves apart if for no other reason than
sanity. I noticed then an actual tendency, when I felt
antagonistic toward Don, unconsciously to identify him
with the dangers and hardships of the mountain; both
opposed me, both were a kind of enemy. Only a tendency, of course, but a frightening one, when I realized
what I was doing. We lacked the balance that the

presence of others could lend to the human situations, so that we could distinguish them from the factors over which we had no control. The mere fact that there were four of us this year tripled the possible relationships and added an inconceivable richness of communication, which made it possible for us to relax.

So I greatly enjoyed the first days camping with Don. It was a pleasure, if a frustrating one, to watch his fine mechanical mind at work, building or fixing something. He had a way of planning that overlooked no detail, a sense of orientation that once, on Deborah, had come in especially handy. We had been forced by the crevasse accidents to hike out via the Susitna Glacier, a route we had never anticipated, and one that lay off our maps. We had been going slowly along the side of the glacier, approaching a particularly bad slope we would have to traverse. Don pointed out a pass above us that, as far as I could tell, led aimlessly off into the foothills. He seemed to remember, from having glanced at a map in Cambridge five months earlier, that the pass would lead us out, short-cutting the bad slope along the glacier that we at least knew would eventually lead where we wanted to get. I was skeptical, but Don talked me into it. The pass was easy; it took us in a straight line in the right direction, and saved us a day which, since we eventually ran out of food, might have been crucial.

Don was tremendously strong, and could summon reserves, when he had to, as on that forced hike out, that one could expect from few men. That strength, combined with his carefulness, gave me a confidence climbing with him that was extremely valuable in crisis. And the loyalty to him that I felt after Deborah, once the antagonism had worn off, fed those quenchless fires of nostalgia that will for a long time raise up visions of all the stretches of the Hayes Range which, till now, he and I are the only men ever to have seen. I will never be able to picture those places empty, as they are now and have been since we left them. I have always seen Don there, his strong arms chopping a step on precipitous ice, his calm eyes looking into a storm-choked sunset, squinting against the wind flung from the turbulent north.

On July 4, the same day we finished the hauling, Matt, Don, and I started to explore the steep, crevassed section of icefall above base camp that lay between us and the face. To begin the real climbing, we had to reach a pass, which we called simply "the col," between Huntington and a small peak to the west. The connecting ridge joined the face two-fifths of the way up, where it merged completely into it. But we would have to climb that lower, jagged ridge to get to the face itself. The ridge was a blessing, however. It was what divided the avalanches from above and made the route less than suicidal. Moreover, it divided the upper branch of the glacier from a much lower one, and we knew that the col, so gently approachable (through the icefall) from this side, overlooked a frightful drop on the other. Now, as the three of us reconnoitered, Ed stayed at base camp nursing a bad blister. The icefall, though easy, was far from trivial. We managed to get all the way through it on snow-shoes, but had to make some ingenious, steep traverses beside some of the bigger crevasses. Halfway through the icefall, I happened to turn around, and found McKinley staring over my shoulder, incredibly high above us. It was our first view of it since landing.

Don took over the lead for the last bit to the col. He was able to make three tricky snowshoe steps right up to the very top of it. Before Matt or I could get there, he let out an involuntary "Wow!" When we got to the col we saw why; we looked over a 3,000-foot gulf. We couldn't even see the bottom; mist was whipping by as the wind reached us, and all we could sense was an uncontainable space beneath our feet. The feeling was sudden and vivid enough so that I didn't really feel comfortable standing up, especially on snowshoes. The col was scarcely big enough for the three of us.

We started down to tell Ed about our progress. There, on the col, the serious climbing would begin. At last we would be getting somewhere. The sudden exposure had both excited and sobered us. None of us had ever come upon a cliff quite so unwarned. It was as if one got up in the morning, had a cup of coffee, and opened the front door to go to work to find his house was an airplane in flight.

5 ▲ Twenty Days'
Despair

The jagged ridge had been the unknown factor on our route, since none of Washburn's photos showed it well. We had anticipated little trouble on it, though, because it was less steep than the face above. Now we weren't so sure. In the first place, large cornices studded every foot of the ridge, overhanging lips of snow that the wind had spent all winter building up and that were destined to collapse within a month. Moreover, all the cornices hung over the near side, so that the moment we began climbing on the ridge we would have to stay slightly below its crest on the other side, with that awful 3,000-foot gulf, in which the darkness seemed to gather and linger, constantly beneath our feet.

We divided the ridge with three names. The first, long, jagged section of it became the "Stegosaur," for its resemblance to the spiny monster that had flourished while the ridge was being formed. Above that we distinguished two steep snowfields, set sideways to the ridge, as the "Lower" and "Upper Parks." Connecting them was a 100-foot ice gully, the "Alley." We hoped in two or three days to reach the Alley, and from there to spend a day crossing the Upper Park, above which rose the face, monolithic, ominous.

But the first problem was simply to get started. On July 5, we carried a light load through the icefall and split into two pairs at the col to try different approaches. Matt and Ed went a quarter-mile closer to the face, beneath the ridge, to try to climb a steep ice wall, tunnel straight through a cornice, and thereby short-cut some of the Stegosaur. Don and I started right at the col. He belayed from the safe side while I led. For thirty feet I could simply walk to the top of a little snow plume. But to continue I had to climb down the back side of it, which was vertical for ten feet. One of the rough maxims of climbing says that snow cannot adhere at more than a 55-degree angle; but snow that undergoes the torture of the wind and cold of big mountains finds that it must disobey the maxim to survive. The little plume I now stood on was the first of many incredible snow and ice features we were to meet on Huntington. I started down the back side of it, trying to kick steps into the crumbly snow with my crampons. Suddenly, a few feet below me, a huge section of cornice broke. Watching it, I had the impression I was riding on top of it. Since it fell on the gentle side of the ridge, it went only a hundred feet; but the pulverizing power of that short fall, of tons of rotten ice sloughing to a halt, was frightening, especially since we had thought the cornices were more stable than that and had been considering pitching a camp under one. I quickly retreated to Don. We were both thinking of Matt and Ed, getting ready to tunnel through just such a cornice. Quickly we circled beneath the ridge, following their steps; we met them just as they were starting up the ice wall below the cornice. Not wishing to alarm them, Don said, "It looks a bit too warm today, guys. We had a little cornice break off near us, so maybe we should wait for better conditions."

Matt looked disappointed; Ed looked as if he were saying to himself, "What are they trying to tell us?" But they gave up the effort and returned with us to the col. When they saw the debris of the broken cornice, they were alarmed. Cornices look so graceful in position that it is easy to forget their tremendous weight and the ugly force with which they can collapse.

Convincing ourselves that the problem was only a matter of temperatures, we decided to spend the rest of the day digging a snow cave just below the col. With our two shovels we started into a 15-degree slope. Just below the surface the snow became the hard, chunky sort that makes a good cave. To me the digging was simply hard work, but Ed loved it, and insisted on doing all the shoveling himself. That was all right with the rest of us; we leaned on our axes and looked at the route.

Despite our bravado, it was a terrible beginning. If we had to abandon a day's effort after thirty feet, how long would it take us to climb the thousands of feet that lay above us? The collapsing cornice seemed like a stern rebuke. The mountain might have been saying, "What do you foolish boys think you're doing here? Go home before you get hurt."

Mountaineers can't afford to be superstitious, though they often are. Perhaps a superstitious kind of feeling made Don and me begin to think, as we looked at the route, that perhaps the best way to start the climbing would be to go directly through the debris of the recent collapse. Of course there were logical reasons for it as well. That was the spot where the least overhanging snow remained, and cornices, more exhaustible than lightning, seldom strike twice in the same place. Since Ed was taking care of the cave, Don decided to try it. The short wall of recently fractured ice gave him problems; it was almost vertical, and parts of it were very loose. Don came down to let Matt, who was carrying some ice screws, have a try. Putting one of the screws in for protection near the top of the cliff, Matt felt safe enough to start tunneling through the snow. Soon we saw his head appear on the other side of the ridge. Ed and I cheered. Matt continued forty feet to a pillar of rock. As he reached it, the three of us apprehensively watched. It would be the first time we had been able to examine the rock anywhere in the basin; on its solidity probably depended all our chances of success. Matt touched the pillar and looked it over, not saying anything. Then he took a piton and began to hammer it into a crack. As the pitch of the pounded metal rose and began to ring like a bell, we cheered again. Matt returned, confirming our guess: the rock was a superb, sharp-edged granite. We went back down to base camp in much better spirits. Not only had the rock lived up to our highest expectations, but we had turned the first battle, which had looked like a rout, into a fair contest. From far down the icefall we could look back and see the beautiful tunnel Matt had dug, the most visible sign of climbing progress we could dent the mountain with.

The next day Don and I got an early start; by 4:30 A.M. we were advancing the route. The going was consistently difficult, but in half an hour Don had climbed a pitch of steep ice, and reached a spot from which he could belay me up. We were always able to get solid pitons in the rock for belays, so that we felt a certain sense of security despite the drop below us. The day was cold and perfect. In the sun on the South Buttress of McKinley, every speck of snow stood out; though it was seven miles away, we fancied that we could have seen a person standing on it. However, as I followed Don's steps in the steep ice, my head brushed the slope, knocking my glasses off. They went the way of every snowslide, probably to the very floor of the glacier. Fortunately I had another pair at base camp, but for the rest of the day I couldn't see very well. I led another pitch, then brought Don up to try what looked like the hardest bit yet. For twenty minutes he made no headway, having to clear masses of crusty snow out of the way to get to the ice-covered rock below. Then he was able to progress at a very slow rate, hanging on to pitons, inching up the slippery rock. So far, we had climbed only at night since the snow got too unstable during the day. Now, as I stood in shadow belaying Don only a few feet away, I got miserably cold. Climbing often involves that kind of inequality; since only one man can move at a given time, the belayer may nearly freeze while the climber gets overheated. Cold has a capacity to heighten loneliness, too. I know of few lonelier occupations than belaying when one is cold; one's partner is out of sight, and all one can gauge his progress by is the slow paying out of the rope. At least I could watch Don, this time, though the absence of my glasses made it hard to see what he was doing. At last, at the end of an hour, he had gained a ledge forty feet up. He put in a piton, attached a fixed rope; then we descended. All the way up the route we were to leave these light, cheap ropes in, since it was the only way to make reasonably safe all the difficult pitches we would have to climb again with loads, several times each. We had brought nearly 7,000 feet of fixed rope; we eventually used it all.

When we got back to the col we found Matt and

Ed at work on our cave. It looked very good, with a combination hall and foyer inside the door, and the beginnings of a bedroom to the right. Even when it was sunny outside, though, a perpetual cold reigned within the cave, for the subsurface snow never warms, much less melts, in Alaska. Don and I went down to base camp; Matt and Ed would spend that night in the cave in order to get a good start on the route the next day.

That evening Sheldon flew over a half-dozen times, circling low over our tent at base camp. He also flew over the gap of the col, so he probably saw our steps leading up there and perhaps also signs of digging around the snow cave. Don and I waved at Sheldon, and wondered if he was trying to tell us something. But what could he possibly tell us? If the world had declared war, if New York City were gone, we wouldn't find out till after the expedition.

Around 1:30 A.M. I woke from a drowsy sleep to hear faint shouts. My first thought, given substance by a bad dream I had been having, was "They are in trouble." As I shook off the sleepiness I realized that the shouts were simply their belay signals yelled back and forth. That was good—it meant they were off to an early start and should get a lot of the Stegosaur climbed today. But later, when Don and I arrived at the col, we found that Matt and Ed, despite a full day's work, had been unable to place more than two new pitches. Ed's pitch, our fifth, was especially difficult. He climbed a cliff of the steepest ice we had yet

▲ 73

found (about 80 degrees), directly beneath a prow of rock he deftly bypassed. Six pitches in three days—less than half the Stegosaur, less than a fourth of the ridge, less than a—what?—tenth? of the whole route. So far, moreover, the climbing had been difficult; yet the face above was bound to be even harder. We were beginning to get discouraged.

Don and I had enlarged the snow cave with a bedroom on the left, and that night all four of us slept in it for the first time. The plan was for Don and me to advance the route that night, while Matt and Ed brought a load up from base camp. But when Don and I got up to go there was a white-out. It was warm, but a wind blew stinging snow over the col: insidious weather, the worst possible for the route. We went back to bed. Later, all four of us descended to base camp and brought up heavy loads in the horrible, sloppy snow that the unusual warmth was making of our icefall route. As we neared the cave again, we could hear the hiss of wet piles of snow sliding off the ridge above, effacing the steps it had taken us so long to chop and kick.

That night, July 8–9, we resolved to make the strongest possible attack on the route, one pair starting at midnight, the other relieving them four hours later. But the weather, still poor, began to get worse. When Matt and Don awoke at midnight it was actually raining. They could hear, but not see, structures collapsing not only on our route but all over the basin. Going would have been pointless and quite dangerous. At

4:00 A.M. Ed and I had a look, but things were as bad as before. So we declared our first rest day and tried to enjoy it. During the day, the temperature rose higher than we were to record again for the balance of the expedition, to an incredible 46° F. But at the same time it was a chilly 16° F. in the cave. Still, the amount of space we had in it was a virtue no usable tent possesses; each of the two bedrooms was roughly the size and shape of the inside of a small car. What was more, we didn't have to keep it clean. We read a lot, wrote in our diaries, cooked delicacies, like stewed banana flakes, and broke open our one recreational luxury—a Monopoly set. We propped the board on some food boxes in the kitchen so that we could easily play from the bedrooms; only the banker ever had to sit up. It would have been hard to play Monopoly in our tent except by remote control, and then the possibilities for cheating would have been irresistible. I like to think we had other reasons for building the cave, but this turned out to be its greatest advantage.

Perhaps, though, the cave was a way for us to hide from the route. At the time we might have felt such an urge; and the cave's isolation was certainly total. We could barely hear an airplane flying by, even straining; someone shouting at the top of his voice could not be heard outside more than thirty feet away. The snow let some light through, but most of our illumination came from the door; yet only from a single angle could one see anything out the door but a patch of sky. But the cave engendered in us no claustrophobia. Perhaps we

▲ 75

did want to hide. It has since intrigued me to think of the cave—sealed up by winter snows shortly after we left it, an empty tomb gradually sinking within the glacier, intact, as the new snows of each successive year pile above it; some three hundred cubic feet of space, once a place that briefly housed four men's fears and hopes; whose walls once absorbed laughter, the rattle of dice, the roar of a stove, the nervous swish of a pencil writing; where still lie a few discarded books, an empty food can, a sock with a hole in the toe, a Monopoly set—that will never be seen again by any man. We lived there for a month as alert to the few things we chose for a while to make our lives as we were oblivious to all the rest. The snow cave was cold as a freezer, west of our mountain—so we called it the Westing House. As we lay within it the only visible sign of our presence from outside would have been the small hole in the snow that served as our door. Had an avalanche swept over us, we would have slept through it, never awakening. Had the Battle of Gettysburg been fought just below us on the Tokositna, we might have heard the occasional faint pop of the cannon. An existentialist dream (or nightmare), our cave, the perfect realization of man's essential solitude, which was discovered in the twentieth century among the crowds in Paris and New York, though men have been as alone as glaciers and galaxies since they learned to think. Yet the cave did not oppress us; with a grunt we could communicate. There was no telephone to answer, the supermarket was just outside the door, and the library at the foot of the sleeping bag was open twenty-four hours a day. For a while we were self-sufficient; but that is all one can say, anyway, since men die. No Utopia, our snow cave; ours was no society, or, if one, its only stratum was the ruling class, four smug kings. No spiritual pilgrimage, our snowshoe hike up there; no quest of truth more apocalyptic than a handhold, our climbing above. At least it is easy to say that; but at the last disavowal I want to hesitate. After all, it would be nice to believe that climbing could somehow be a search for truth as well as for a summit. Or, if one assumes that life itself is that kind of search, it would be nice to believe that climbing could actually find something. It would somehow justify the effort. This part of Mount Huntington was, of course, a new place on the earth, and in the age that has doomed the geographical unknown, mountaineering can be regarded as a final twist of exploration. The sides of steep mountains are perhaps the hardest places on the earth to reach. But is a two-inch crack in a granite slab in the middle of an economically useless cliff even of geographical interest? Yet we, the four of us, could thrill to see even a one-inch crack. As long as men had been confined to the earth's surface, there was still the allure of hidden places; there were still "Shangri-La's" and "Golden West's" in their minds, at least. But the airplane ended that; it proved that the world looks pretty much the same all over; big places and cold places exist, of course, but the pattern is the same: there are only seas and deserts, jungles and forests, plains and mountains, swamps and icecaps. The airplane proved, above all, that you didn't have to be there to find out what a place was like. There are still plenty of square miles of land on which no man has ever stood; but before someone does, he will probably consult a map that can tell him where to dig for tungsten, or how many feet, give or take a few, the rain that falls there must roll to reach the sea. No, the place for explorers now is space; what mountain wall can stir the exploratory imagination as can the Plutonian desert?

There are on mountains, of course, summits. But the only pot of gold is at the end of the Pikes Peak Hill Climb. The summits one may now visit before anyone else looks remarkably like other parts of their mountains. The air is the same as, if a little thinner than, that at the bottom; the snow there would melt in one's hand to the same dreary water that flows from its foot. No ladder leads into the sky, and to try to get higher would be as futile for the climber as it was for Icarus. Men, among them mountaineers, have claimed that the only discovery one can make by climbing is that of oneself. But there must be easier ways; and anyway, is that discovery as important as others we might attempt with the same effort? Will it cure loneliness? Will it make death sweet? Yet I have come down from mountains comprehending no better who I am or why I climbed than when I set out, and still been happy. Climbers take risks, and to climb is so all-involving that it temporarily approximates life. If the old question, the one Mallory tried to answer is a valid one, I have given up trying to meet it rationally. Perhaps, if one were immortal, he would feel prompted to ask an ordinary person "Why do you live?" How well could that embarrassed mortal answer? Beyond the neatness of any rationale for life lies its untranslatable glory, the elemental courage of wanting to live. Climbing is serious, because it is like life for us who do it, not like a sport; perhaps we betray it by trying to explain our reasons.

The next night, July 9–10, only Don and I planned to climb. We got off an hour late, but surprisingly both the weather and the condition of the snow were superb. Thanks to the fixed ropes, we reclimbed the six pitches without belaying in only one hour. I led our first new pitch, on which we ran into the first of many "chute-tops," the steep upper bowls of the funnel-like gullies, whose treacherous snow had to be traversed in order to reach the next tower of rock. We were on a more or less level stretch now; the Stegosaur wound its tortuous way ahead of us, spine after spine gapped by the chute-tops. We were always tempted to climb on the sure, solid rock, but we knew that once we had steps placed in the snow and ice they would be much easier to follow with loads than pitches on the difficult rock. The climbing became spectacular, without being terribly difficult; but the unusualness of the terrain made us uneasy. Always beneath us gaped that incredible gulf, which, in good weather, we could see was made of ice-plated rock and steep, plastered snow scarred by the grooves of avalanches and the dents of falling rocks. After two more pitches we grew optimistic about finishing the Stegosaur in a day or two. But we had to turn back, then; despite our fine time, we were beginning to get far enough above the cave so that it took too long to cross the previous pitches in order to start the next ones. We had to find a camp site soon, but so far nothing had looked remotely usable. Bivouacs, or tentless camps, tend to be a last resort in Alaska because of the arctic cold and the danger of getting caught in a long storm.

The weather stayed clear all day. We decided to try the shift system that night. Don and Matt tried to get to sleep early, but Ed and I could bask in the sun outside. We were sitting on two food cans reading when Sheldon flew over. We stood up and waved; to our surprise he responded by dropping a box out his window.

Excitedly we waited for it to land. It looked at first as if it would hit somewhere below us in the middle of the icefall. I started to complain about having to hike down to pick it up, but Ed said, "No, look, it's sailing up toward us."

After a moment I said, "Yeah, you're right. Wouldn't it be funny if it sailed right on over the col?"

With a whoosh the box flew over our heads and disappeared just beyond the col. Ed howled with disappointment. We ran up to the col. I thought I could pick out a scrape in the snow, just twenty feet below the crest, where the box must have hit before taking

photo courtesy of Bradford Washburn

1. Mt. Huntington from the west-northwest, French Ridge in the center.

photo courtesy of Bradford Washburn

2. The upper part of the west face of Mt. Huntington. The route is marked in the solid line, with camps II (Alley Camp), IIa (temporary), III (Nose Camp), and IV (Bivouac). The French route is the left-hand sky line.

photo by Don Jensen

3. Fog over the Tokositna Glacier. Visible in the left foreground is part of the south ridge of Mt. Huntington; beyond it, an unnamed spur of Mt. Hunter.

4. Ed Bernd standing beside Alley Camp. The south ridge of Mt. Huntington is in the background, and fog covers the lower Tokositna Glacier. Note ropes tying tent to the ice.

photo by Don Jensen

5. The author belaying at the top of the ninth pitch, on the Stegosaur. Cornices are visible at left.

6. Matt Hale standing beneath the Nose. Note the fixed rope indicating where the overhang was climbed.

photo by Don Jensen

7. Ed Bernd belaying at the top of the 38th pitch, having just traversed a steep snow-ice slope, on the summit day.

photo by Don Je[rman]

8. Sunrise on the summit of Mt. Huntingt[on].
Left to right: Bernd, Roberts, Hale.

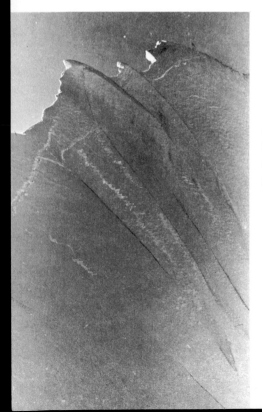

photo by David Roberts

9. Looking back at the summit and the summit ri[dge]
on the descent. The left-hand edge
is heavily corniced. Note the steps and fixed rope.

photo by Don Je[rman]

10. The author, just three pitches bel[ow]
the summit, on the desce[nt]

photo by Don Jensen

11. Ed Bernd rappelling off the Nose on the descent. Note fixed line with loops left on the pitch.

the 3,000-foot plunge. We returned to the cave, waking Don and Matt to complain about the tragedy.

"What if it was the radio?" Matt blurted sleepily. I had a vision of trying to explain it to the rental company, as a squad of private detectives held guns on us to make us sign away five years' labor to pay it off. Sheldon, of course, couldn't be held responsible. After the expedition we found out our sympathetic pilot had tried to supply us with a gallon of ice cream. "Marshmallow ripple, too," he said wistfully.

Despite the excitement, Don and Matt got off by midnight. The weather was deteriorating. When Ed and I arose four hours later, a gray cloud bank was blowing in from the south. Before we caught up with the other two, we heard their shouted signals, mingled with the unnerving sound of big rocks crashing down. When we got nearer, we could see Matt leading across a dike of black, basaltic rock, the only bad rock on our route. The patch of red, Matt's parka, against the blackness seemed tiny and ineffectual, especially because Don's belay spot was hidden around a corner so it looked, though we knew better, as if Matt were going it alone. They had four new pitches placed by the time we caught them; more important, they had finished the Stegosaur. Ed and I took over the lead at the bottom rim of the Lower Park. Climbing on a smooth expanse of steep snow, though easy, rattled me at first. The protective solidity the rock had offered was gone. After bringing Ed up the first pitch, I asked him if I could lead the next one as well. Since I weighed about fifty pounds less than he, it would be safer that way. He was very generous. As I led off and glanced back, nothing could have looked solider than that rock of a belayer. More than his size, his cheerfulness gave him that look of strength that I relied on. That cheerfulness was an element we would have totally lacked without him; it was one element Don and I had missed on Deborah. There Ed stood now, facing into the wind, shivering, but he was grinning. He was enjoying it.

Ed seemed born for that sort of contradictory challenge, for battlefields bigger than those his will could rule. His uncharacteristic depression in our first week on the glacier, or the long hours on the road he had insisted on staying awake, watching, brooding in the night, as if his life were bound to be short and had to be lived hard, as if sleep were its betrayal, seemed to resolve now into the happiness he could find only in climbing. I knew how he felt; I felt as he did the sting of the cold, knowing as he did that the cold could not really get to us, and that in the face of the gray storm that was approaching we could continue to climb, for a while at least, each footstep penetrating farther into a place man had never gone. I knew the wild, close feeling in his heart that welcomed even the wind; the very act of standing before it a declaration that this was part of what he was meant to live for—or if not meant (if there had been no intention in his creation), then at least it was one of those few things that he could momentarily devote all of himself to, body, heart, mind, without the need for anything else. But I could also hear with him the mind's whispered warning not to climb too bravely or too far, which seemed to echo from the spiritless gulf beneath our feet. I knew all this, but only because I felt it, too. The rest of Ed, how he differed from me, I could scarcely glimpse.

The Lower Park had some bad snow on it. The top of the fourteenth pitch was the first belay spot where we couldn't place a rock piton. I had tried to use one of the special long aluminum daggers we had made for soft ice and snow, but only after burying it and waiting for it to freeze in did I feel confident of its stability. We placed a total of two and a half new pitches before the wind, rising to a gale and flinging snow in our faces, forced us to return. It had been our best day yet. Together, the four of us had got nearly seven new pitches in. As we reached the cave, our hair and eyelashes crusted with ice, Ed and I felt a tired satisfaction. But we had still seen no camp site above and we had to have one soon.

We learned that Don, in descending, had banged his head on his ice ax quite hard. He suffered headaches and spells of seeing double for several weeks afterward; but if he had a concussion, it didn't hinder his climbing. The storm increased that day and the temperature rose. There was no chance of climbing again the next night, so we got all our clothes as dry as we could in the cave. Our consciences wouldn't let us waste a day, so we descended to base camp for a load in the morning, getting our clothes soaked again. The cave was particularly miserable to enter wet; it must have been a little like going into a walk-in freezer after a shower.

The encouragement of our good day waned and died, as a four-day storm besieged us. Every night we woke and prepared to climb, but the weather and warmth frustrated all our efforts. On July 14 Ed and Matt started at 3:00 A.M. Don and I were going to follow later, but the other two made terribly slow progress, getting wet and tired rechopping all the steps. They managed to climb only the first four pitches. They left their loads there, but it was a wasted day. Don and I never started.

Two days later the weather seemed to improve, and the temperature dropped to 26° F. We had begun to feel the time pressure; we were way behind schedule, and we couldn't hold out much beyond August 10. Therefore we decided we had to force things. Don and I started out first to clear the route. Matt and Ed followed with the bare minimum of a camp, determined to pitch it somewhere above. All the steps were gone; the four-day storm had filled them up or avalanched them off. But despite the slow going, the snow was at last crisp again. Don and I reached our previous high point in four hours, and after two more we had placed our eighteenth and nineteenth pitches, almost to the end of the Lower Park. On the way down we passed Ed and Matt, who were bringing up their camp. Though we didn't know it then, the four of us would never camp together again, and we would never climb together until the summit day. The clear weather that seemed in the offing had deteriorated; as we continued down, the snow began to fall heavily. Near the bottom one of my crampons broke; as the last straw, our spare pair was at base camp, which we'd hoped not to have to visit again. Now there was no choice but to make another wet trip down the icefall the next day.

Meanwhile Matt and Ed had reached the top of our highest pitch. There was a possibility there for a camp site, but a poor one. Leaving their loads, they pushed the route higher to look for a better spot. At the top of the Lower Park Matt led into the steep ice chute of the Alley, then nicely around the corner onto the Upper Park. They were exhilarated by the easy going above; quickly they stormed up five more pitches, but the steep slope never relented. Disappointed, they gave up the search and went back down. They were getting tired after a long day, and the storm's fury continued to increase. At last, in the afternoon, they reached their packs again. They set to work chopping a tent platform out of the 45-degree ice. It was frightfully slow work. After five hours they had a ledge large enough to accommodate the small tent, though for safety they had to pass ropes that were anchored to pitons around it and prop a rock under one of the outside corners. At midnight, near exhaustion after nineteen straight hours of work, they piled into the tent. They had four days of food there, and hoped to push the route further, but they absolutely depended on support from below.

Down in the cave, Don and I were getting discouraged. The storm continued. We spent the next day, as anticipated, retrieving the extra crampons, but the snow conditions were so poor we couldn't have climbed anyway. On July 18 we started up with a load. Don, leading, had to plow away deep masses of sticky snow. We were trying to climb continuously, but this was not possible while the snow prevented us from seeing each other. As Don led, the rope between us would bite into the new snow and stick. Don would feel the rope taut behind him and stop, thinking that I was on a hard stretch. I would see the rope cease to move above me and stop also, assuming Don was on a difficult move or clearing away some snow. So we would both stand there until one of us would impatiently shout, "Are you climbing?"

After a pause the other voice would trickle back: "No! Are you on a hard move?"

"No."

"Climb, then!"

"The rope is stuck!"

"Where?"

The situation was impossible. The shouting only made us irritable with each other. We gave up on the fourth pitch, tied our loads to a piton and returned to the cave. Waiting there was even worse. We kept worrying about Matt and Ed. For all we knew they'd never been able to pitch a tent, but were huddled miserably somewhere, tied to some rock, waiting out the storm. The natural gloominess of the cave enhanced our fears. Matt and Ed were out of sight, out of earshot, and apparently out of safe climbing distance so long as the storm continued. They had only four days of food. We knew they would start to ration it, if necessary, but it wouldn't stretch much beyond six days. Having to ration, moreover, was the first step toward emergency.

In addition, we were getting nowhere on the route. Always present in our minds was the experience of Don and me on Deborah, when day after day of storms, during which we couldn't leave the tent, ate away our chances until, when the weather finally cleared, there was no hope left. Yet that year after twenty days we were halfway up. We had been on Huntington twenty days, but now we were less than a third of the way to the top, with all the real difficulties ahead of us.

On July 19 we forced ourselves to reach Matt and Ed. All the steps needed replacing, even those we had chopped the day before. Our progress was extremely slow; with 40-pound packs we had to make brutal efforts to climb some of the pitches. The snow was still falling. When, leading on the seventeenth pitch, I caught sight of the little triangle of orange above, seemingly tacked to the wall, I felt a thrill of relief. By the time we reached the tent it seemed silly ever to have worried.

Matt and Ed, however, had been unable to get out of their camp since pitching it. The exposure was fantastic. The front door looked straight across the face to the ghostly south ridge of Huntington, and inches from the door the slope swept sheer almost 4,000 feet to the lower glacier. Anything dropped out of the tent apparently went all the way; we lost a pot that way when somebody nudged it.

But their achievement in the face of all these problems cheered us up. Don stayed with Ed in the tent, while Matt descended with me. The weather got steadily better, and the sun actually peeked out occasionally. As we passed the ninth pitch I looked over the side of the ridge where a cornice had broken back to the bare ice. I'd had a hunch that it might be less than a full rope-length down to a high tongue of glacier below. If so, we could set up a rappel rope here for descending, and, on the way up, climb the rope by the prusik technique, thereby short-cutting the first nine pitches. We dropped a rope over the edge. It reached with thirty feet to spare! Soon the thing was set up, and we had an easy descent to the cave. The next day we prusiked up the rope and hauled our packs. The slope was about 70 degrees, made of hard blue ice over which the packs slid smoothly. We reached the tent with our loads and deposited them. We could hear Ed and Don climbing above the Upper Park. We were particularly anxious to know how they were doing, because at last they were confronting the face itself. On our way down we came in sight of them. They looked very small against the towering wall above. As we watched, it became obvious from their painfully slow movement that the climbing was truly severe. Don had to belay from one spot, a cold and dangerous ledge, for more than three hours.

Just before getting to camp, Matt and I saw a lenticular cloud cap forming on the summit of McKinley, the kind that almost inevitably presages a storm. Therefore, even though it was a fine clear day, we were pessimistic. The pattern proved true to form, for soon a blanket of cloud had enveloped us and snow had begun to fall. The storm continued without change for three days. The long hours in the cave slowly passed with nothing for Matt and me to do but wait and talk. The monotony of the softly falling snow made us wonder if it would ever stop. The storm seemed to be the final blow to our chances, if the intrinsic difficulties Ed and Don had begun to explore hadn't been. In despair Matt and I discussed other possibilities, even that of abandoning the route altogether and trying to salvage something for the summer, like a new route on Hunter. But the dream would be gone. All those months in Cambridge thinking about what would be the hardest route ever done in Alaska, if only we could pull it off, seemed wasted. In the depth of gloom I looked around for someone, something to blame, but all that I had was the exasperating feeling of our inadequacy. The cave always seemed too big for two people; Monopoly had lost its interest, and we spent the long hours reading our soggy books or simply thinking.

At last the storm ended. On July 23 we set out for the Alley Camp, as we had begun to call the tent Don and Ed were occupying. The snow had covered our steps again, and a coating of ice had to be scraped off the rope as we prusiked up. We had hoped Don and Ed might be climbing today, but as we approached the tent it became obvious they were still in it. We met them just as they were getting dinner cooked. They had spent twenty hours desperately trying to fix their stove, which had broken, and at last had got it working again. But if we were to trade places, they had to descend right away. With more than gallantry, they left the cooked dinner for us and packed to go down. The weather, which I'd hoped would at last hold clear for a while, had turned foul again. Snow was falling in a slight wind. As they got ready to leave, Matt and I asked them about their progress on the face. They'd managed only two and a half new pitches in their four days; those had been extreme and strenuous, harder by far than anything on the ridge.

I saw no reason to be encouraged. But Ed was inexplicably enthusiastic. "The climbing's beautiful up there," he said. "We'll make it, Dave. You wait and see." I got annoyed. It irritated me that he didn't see how poor our chances were; I thought it was evidence of poor judgment. Only months later, after the expedition, did I think of that moment again; only then was I reminded of it by recalling that, after all, I had been wrong and Ed right. And only then did I realize how important Ed's enthusiasm, his refusal to give up, had been to all of us. I gradually pieced together again how we had felt at the time, and it became apparent to me that, actually, Ed had been no more optimistic than any of us; without the experience of other expeditions, the difficulties we were facing must have seemed overwhelming to him. I saw that Ed had realized all this, but had sensed the faltering of our morale, and had done the one thing he could to bolster it, had put on the only mask of encouragement we wouldn't see through. It was so characteristic of him, of his almost magical way of understanding people, of his rare talent for knowing when to use tact instead of honesty without being dishonest. I felt empty, realizing this, because it was all too late, because I hadn't told him I understood and thanked him for it. Because I hadn't understood. . . . All he had said was, "We'll make it, Dave."

6 ▲ Blue Sky and Hope

The snow didn't let up on July 24. Matt and I, glad at last to be out of the chilly cave, began to get used to the cramped and careful existence the Alley Camp demanded. We couldn't climb that day; we were getting high enough now so that we could push the route ahead only in good weather, because of the cold and the difficulty of the climbing. We shifted to a daytime schedule for the same reason.

The twenty-fifth dawned perfectly clear. I had no inkling of the fact until I stuck my head out the door and saw blue sky above the savage pinnacles of the south ridge. We got started as quickly as we could, after a hurried breakfast. All our water came from chunks of ice we chopped off the tent platform. Just as we got ready to go, the sun hit the tent. The effect wildly rejuvenated our spirits. We had almost given up believing that the sun ever shone. Now the tent warmed like a greenhouse to a comfortable room temperature, even though it was only 25° F. outside.

As we started up the Alley, we saw how much work we'd have to do simply to restore the easy pitches. The steps had vanished. Only the fixed ropes, which hadn't been placed throughout, showed where the route went. Fortunately Matt remembered the details of the pitches from his first trip up nine days before. We found that by kicking under the new snow we could find the old steps, still pretty solid.

Soon we had crossed the Upper Park. Above us loomed a vertical inside corner of rock, the twenty-sixth pitch, the first one of the face. Don had led it on July 20, climbing the rock free in crampons. When Matt and I tried to reclimb the pitch with 25-pound packs, we realized what an incredible performance Don's had been. We had to take the packs off to climb the pitch, then haul them up when we got to the top. And even though we relied heavily on the fixed rope they'd left, the pitch was a strenuous effort.

Nor was the next one much easier. Ed had led this, also in crampons, up 70-degree slabs that plated the core of the mountain. The intricate pitch wandered off to the left, then back directly over the belayer. This had been where Ed was climbing when we had seen Don belaying from his cold perch for so long. Every bit of ice Ed had to chop out of the cracks had bombarded Don below. Again I found it impossible to carry the light pack over the pitch, even with the help of a fixed rope. The four days of storm between our efforts had coated not only the rock but the ropes with rime-ice and feathers of frost. All of it had to be cleared away. My crampons scraped and slipped on the smooth rock. At one point, I stuck the pick of my ax in a crack above my head and tried to do a pull-up on the ax. Finally, after making the kind of effort that would leave us tired for a day, we had our loads up to Don's and Ed's previous high point. It had taken six hours. Here Ed had hoped for a camp site, but the possibilities looked very poor to me. We had time only for a tentative half-pitch more before we had to descend. From our highest point we saw Ed and Don far below, climbing on the ridge. But they were on the lower part of the Stegosaur. Matt and I couldn't figure it out. Were they stubbornly refusing to use our short cut? We yelled to them; because the air was perfectly still, we could understand what they yelled back:

"We're cleaning the first nine pitches."

Thus we learned that Don and Ed were ascending the first pitches a last time to remove the pitons and fixed ropes from them. If we got a chance for the summit, we would need all the equipment above. It was a thankless chore, especially on a beautiful day. But they had had the lead for a while; now they were supporting us.

94 ▲

Matt and I returned to the tent, our muscles sore and tired. The weather was still perfect; we had enjoyed finally getting high on a day when we could see all the way to the horizon. But the fact that it had taken us six hours simply to repeat the previous pitches was pretty discouraging. We could attribute a lot of our slowness to the accumulation of snow and ice from the recent storm. But we would have to go a lot faster the next time to have a hope of putting in any new route.

It was beginning to get dark at night now, not pitch dark, but too dark to read in the tent for a few hours around midnight. Now that we were on a daytime schedule, the darkness helped re-establish for us a diurnal regularity. Because we were still quite pessimistic, though, and because we were tired from the day before, we half hoped for a storm the next day, as an excuse to rest.

But the twenty-sixth also dawned astonishingly clear, and the air stood still around us. We got moving by 10:30 A.M. We decided to carry only the bare minimum of pitons and ropes we would need to put in the route; no extra food, no camp, no equipment for farther up. The snow, thanks to the sun on it yesterday and the night's freeze, was in beautiful shape. We flew over the ten old pitches in two hours, only a third of what it had taken us yesterday. Matt led the rest of the new pitch we'd taken a stab at before. It forced him into a steep, ice-filled chimney. Sometimes I could see a foot or a hand; sometimes only the rope disappearing into the chimney. Matt was having trouble with it, especially because of the ice. Near the top he ran into a bulge that stuck out over his head, barring further progress. At last he managed to hammer a piton into it, hang a little rope ladder, called a "stirrup," from the piton, and climb past the bulge. Only the next day, when we found the piton loose, did we realize that he'd hammered it not between rock and rock, but between rock and ice; the ice had since melted under the pressure and sun.

Matt's lead was a fine one, but it had taken most of an hour. At this rate we couldn't get much farther, unless we were willing to climb late into the night. But my lead went easier. Though we were climbing now on 60-degree rock and ice, with a 4,500-foot drop below us, the going was not as hard as it had been. For the first time on the expedition, at least for me, the climbing had become an unmixed pleasure.

At times like those, the mind does not wander, nor does it really think, except to make the almost automatic judgments of route, piton, and rope the climbing calls for. One's actions seem to take on something of a pagan ritual: the feet develop sensitivities one would have never thought them capable of; the hands and eyes control one's being. I tend to remember that day, July 26, in these mindless, immediate terms. My memories still rest in my nerve endings, as if in recalling our climbing I could turn my body inside out to examine it under colder light than the sun's. While I was leading that day, I was most acutely aware of the pleasure of contrast in my fingers between the cold give of the snow

and the warm dryness of the rock, between the smooth
ice and the rough granite. More than to anything else,
my fingers were sensitive to the rock; they moved
quickly over it, learning its shape better than my eyes
could, settling instinctively in the right grip. While
I belayed Matt, only my fingers handled the rope
through muffling mittens; then the pleasure was visual:
all our belay spots allowed us to look outward. No
perusal could exhaust the teeming wealth of that sight
of the Tokositna Glacier and the mountains across it
as no one had ever seen them before. Flutings, flashing
in the sun, crowded my view; crevasses scored the glacier below like wrinkles on old skin; even the sky
seemed less rich than those mountains. I could tilt my
head back to watch Matt above, and while I did so
I could feel with his fingers, know with his brain how
far he could lean or reach without losing the precious
edge of balance.

But this kind of remembrance numbs the mind's conscious part, the part that wants to understand as well
as sense. It cannot explain why the touch and strain of
ice and rock under my hands should send pleasure as
well as blood surging through my veins. When most
of our lives are spent dulling our senses in order to
think, ignoring pain in order to tolerate it, how then
could Matt or I wish for a chance only to feel? It
would not have satisfied us, obviously, to sit on some
safe sundeck idly pawing a few chunks of rock and ice
for our sensual amusement. The mind can never really
feel, nor can it stop thinking. Nor was my mind numb

then, I know; in fact, part of the breathless urgency of that day's climbing for me came from another kind of awareness, a detached knowledge that came only from my mind; a sense that the universe was looking over our shoulders, even though all we could see looking back at it was the blank sky's blueness. I tried, then, momentarily to abstract the sensual splendor of our climbing by standing at some metaphorical distance from it. And the farther I got, the more discomforting its smallness and ours seemed. Huntington itself, huge enough only for our minds to encompass, occupied but a little plot of earth in the sprawl of Alaska, which in turn began to cover only a patch on a globe we have made aeronautically puny without figuring out how to leave it. Suppose, however, that we do figure that out; can we ever stand on the sun? The earth would span only an average sun-spot; Huntington less than a speck in the sun-spot; someone climbing Huntington not even a speck on the speck. Yet none of our fondest fantasies, granting us a star's strength or size, seem to realize what we could do with that power. Even our wish for immortality only betrays the limits of our imagination. Matt and I felt a kind of power that day, climbing well in the sun, yet we would be vaporized to a wisp of gas in one instantaneous flick of one infinitesimal tongue of the sun's fire. And the sun, for all its brilliance, is a mediocre star, as stars go (and they are definitely going). Compared even to its prodigal size, moreover, there is so much emptiness around it that the sun might run wild all its life looking for friends, and never bump into another sol. Even this appalling emptiness might leave room for us to proclaim our purpose, since all the stars we can see at night, and quite a few more, belong to one happy galactic society. They all revolve, in orderly paths in the same direction, about the old kings in the center. We might then be no more than the serfs of serfs, but we should know our rulers. But someone had to find out about forty years ago (and the world hasn't been the same since) that some of the things up there were foreigners, apparently oblivious to our galaxy. All of a sudden someone else realized that there were lots of them, and that each of them was not simply an uninvited outlaw, but a whole galaxy of its own. It got worse and worse, as knowledge tends to. It soon became obvious that the distances between galaxies dwarfed the distances between the stars into comparative inches. And, as if space were still not big enough for them, the galaxies seemed to be running away from each other. There is not even a known center; it is not as if all the other galaxies were running away from us; we too are getting out of here as fast as we can.

This is not important, perhaps; it is merely true. Perhaps it should even be comforting, for it tends to indicate that loneliness is not simply our mistake, but the condition of the universe. Think, then, of the lost paradise when, as astronomers (fanciful men) would have us believe, everything (because what is flying apart must once have been together), every grain of dust and star, even the atoms that now make us live, was crammed, let us say ten billion years ago, into a primeval ball that would fit nicely in your pocket next to the penknife.

But if we must take it seriously, it is frightening. Perhaps there is no point laying one's soul open to the universe. The sky is blue, trees and grass grow, men live; what more do we need to know? Let us declare, then, that we will ignore the universe—after all, it ignores us.

If on July 26 my eye saw, metaphorically speaking, beyond the dazzling walls of the Tokositna basin into a raw cosmic night, it did not stop me from climbing with Matt that day. The trouble with the deep end of awareness, the honest vision of a soundless everywhere in which there is no up or down, is that everything human shrinks to nothingness before it. Nothing man does will last forever, granted; but still there is something to say about it. People will listen, if no one else will. Someone will see, for instance, a picture of two men beneath a mountain wall, roped together, apparently trying to climb it, and will thrill somewhat as the climbers themselves did, and wonder what it was like for them. The men in those pictures, so calm and proficient they seem to take on some of the mountain's own implacable cold, still are men, men afraid to die and capable of love. Hooded, gaunt, they have their dreads and wishes. For them motion is life, as much as for anyone. The pictures can paralyze only their balanced grace, suspending something that words, which move as they moved, lose. But the men themselves had to move. Climbing is defined by a purposed completion, the summit; yet the best of it is never that final victory, for after that there is only the descent. The best moments lurk in the tension just before success.

That was what then animated Matt and me. For once, we were moving as perfectly as we knew how. For the first time the summit dared whisper in our ears. It might depend on how far we could get that day, on what we should find in the next few hours.

We faced now three choices, alternatives we had known about from the route photos before we came. Matt and I were just below the hardest part of the whole face, no matter which route we took. On the right (we could just see it now) lay a remarkable hollow, a cave within a cave, sheltered by nested overhangs. If we could get there, we might camp in it and eventually traverse even farther right, beyond and above it, heading at last toward the summit along a thin rock rib. But getting to the double cave looked very difficult, and we knew the traverse beyond might be seriously threatened by avalanches. Directly above us rose a long, smooth slab, averaging a frightening 80 degrees. There would be no possibility of climbing it free. But we could see that the pencil-thin cracks in it tended to peter out, leaving blank gaps of smooth rock into which we should not even be able to get pitons. We had expansion bolts, which as a last resort can substitute for pitons, but even so the going would be slow and difficult, maybe impossible. On the left we could see our third alternative. A steep ice gully led up three hundred feet, stopping under a huge "ceiling," an overhang that split the face without a break. Imagine an ant climbing a wall inside a room, then heading out, upside down, across the ceiling. That is what would be required of us for fifty feet, with the aid, of course, of pitons we might hammer into a crack, if there was one in the ceiling.

Those were the choices. After a short discussion Matt and I chose the left-hand route. The ceiling might be the most difficult of all the problems embodied in all three choices, but at least it was a short, one-pitch problem, not a matter of sustained severity. Three pitches took us up the ice gully. As we neared the ceiling, which we had begun to call the "Nose," we could see that something like a crack, perhaps too wide a crack, split it from bottom to top. When we reached the Nose, it was Matt's turn to lead.

He took off his crampons. Fortunately I had been able to get an extraordinarily solid piton in. I felt secure, which, of course, made Matt feel better too. Without much trouble, he pitoned up the wall beneath the ceiling. Then he found that the crucial crack was six inches wide: wider than any of our pitons. A series of small cracks we hadn't been able to see from below offered an alternative; Matt was able to get our smaller pitons in them. I could watch everything simply by looking straight up, where Matt was dangling like a spider over me. It reminded me of ceilings we'd climbed together in New Hampshire and New York, good "practice" climbs we'd called them, on those cider-sweet autumn days or those spring-thaw afternoons.

This was the real thing, now. Matt was climbing skillfully, calmly, but he knew as well as I that the pitch he was leading was the key to the whole face. It was a matter of simply doing what he knew how to, one piton after the other. Soon he was at the lip of the ceiling; then I saw him step out of his last stirrup and disappear above. In a few minutes he was anchored, and yelled for me to come up.

By the time I reached him, we had already been climbing for eight hours, so it was past the time we should have turned back. The sun lay low in the distance over Mount Foraker, and its flawless light tinged the rock above a brownish-gold. Nothing above us looked as difficult as the Nose. It was still a long way to the summit, but it all seemed possible now. Still, we were reluctant to go down, to end our first perfect climbing day, one of the few in our lives. Always we felt as if the hours of sheer splendid sky and sun were shortly numbered; if we slept, the storms, like thieves, could sneak upon us.

We spoke quietly, discussing the route and our chances rather than the bursting sense of triumph we were beginning to feel. Matt was never one to proclaim his feelings; whether out of a residual shyness or simply to counter my often vocal enthusiasm, he always hid his exultation. But he couldn't disguise his intensity; I felt now, in the silence, an electric tension between us, the charged excitement we occasionally got climbing together, as we had in the last few pitches, from a kind of communication in which the motions of our climbing were more eloquent than words, on which, realizing this, we obtruded only the shouted signals we needed for belaying. Neither of us could have reached this place in the sky alone; if we could have, the excitement would have been fraught with loneliness. Because we shared the pleasure now, neither of us could feel lonely. All that was visible of the pleasure in Matt's face was its intensity, the almost haggard gauntness, as if his body itself were ravaged rather than fed by that intensity. I had seen it first on that beginners' climb in New York, again out of a wild storm in New Hampshire, once glowing through a fever on a sharp summit in Colorado, now where it belonged, on a big mountain, a mountain that could match his intensity with cold massiveness.

But we had to go down. We rappelled off the Nose, dangling for the last seventy feet completely in the air, connected only to the rope. Then we descended the long ice gully; we could watch our shadows, projected on the rock wall a hundred feet away, climbing down beside us like a pair of phantom imitators. Then the sun set, and we continued down into the dusk.

On the Upper Park, as it was getting really dark, we met Ed and Don. They were terribly excited. They had seen us climbing way above, but hadn't realized that we'd actually passed the Nose. They intended to go on up that night, looking for a place to camp somewhere above. We assured them there were no good sites until the Nose. They compromised, pitching our other tent at the top of the Upper Park, having to work far into the night to build a platform. Matt and I descended the six pitches to the Alley Camp. We arrived after a twelve-and-a-half-hour day, very tired, very happy.

The next morning an early mist surprised us. But it lifted, revealing another superb day. We had to have another camp above, maybe two, before we could assault the summit. The plan was for Matt and me to carry loads up to the top of the gully just beneath the Nose, where Ed and Don, following, would try to pitch a camp. Matt and I got off in the late morning, but we were still tired, and moved lethargically. We passed Ed and Don as they were starting to take down their tent. Above the twenty-ninth pitch, where Matt and I had left our loads two days before, we picked up the two food boxes and continued. We couldn't wear our packs in the ice-filled chimney; but the set-up of the pitch was so awkward that it took two hours to work out a hauling system on it. Above, things went faster. We got the loads to the Nose at 6:20 P.M. An hour later, going down, we crossed ropes with Ed and Don as they ascended to set up their high camp. The meeting had an emotionality about it that none of our others had had. We all felt a tense joy now that things were working; moreover, as we got higher, the strange and beautiful country of vertical ice and rock more exclusively involved us. Matt and I knew we might not see the other two again before they had reached the summit. We knew, also, that Ed and Don might be the only ones who would have a chance of getting to the top. It didn't matter. Any kind of success, after the storms and dulled hopes of the last months, would fill us with gratitude. As we passed them in the dying sunlight, we couldn't tell them how much our desires went with them; instead we breathlessly described every detail of the route and every item of strategy we thought might aid them. They couldn't tell us how proud and thankful they were for our work getting past the Nose; so they arranged plans for the next few days when we would be out of contact. Thus the meeting, like so many human confrontations, passed in confused inarticulateness, for which only the joy in my throat compensated. I wanted to sit for hours with them, but co-operation now depended on our contrary paths. So Matt and I climbed down into the dusk again as Ed and Don went up into the pure sky.

The next day, July 28, we woke to find the weather still holding, though clouds had begun to build far to the northwest behind McKinley and Foraker. In a short but strenuous day, Matt and I went down to the ninth pitch and retrieved, in one horrible 55-pound load each, the pitons, rope, and food we would need to take up to Don and Ed for the assault above the Nose. That day we never saw or heard them, so we couldn't tell what they had accomplished.

It turned out that the platform beneath the Nose had taken them a very long time to chop, their efforts complicated by finishing in the midnight darkness. The platform was never really adequate for the tent, which had to be pitched narrower than usual. Nor could they get very good pitons into the smooth wall above to anchor the tent. But at least the projecting eave of the Nose above guarded the tent from falling rocks. The front door overlooked the spectacular western drop to the Tokositna basin, and the sun set that night almost in line with the door. Inches beyond its outside wall, the steep snow slope plunged toward vertical rock. Don and Ed were camped above a 5,000-foot drop, down which an object might fall with only five or six bounces. Everything outside the tent—food boxes, fixed ropes, hard hats, hammers—had to be tied to the wall.

Because they hadn't finished the job until early morning, Don and Ed couldn't accomplish much on the twenty-eighth. Don placed a fixed line of stirrups on the Nose, though, so that it could be climbed with less effort than leading it had taken. They needed further support from us below, however. But they were ready the next day to push the route above the Nose, as far as they could, maybe to a point in reach of the summit. If only the weather held. . . .

7 ▲ The Summit

July 29 dawned clear. Our fifth perfect day in a row, it was almost more than we could believe. Don and Ed got moving by 7:30 A.M. Quickly over the Nose, from there on, they faced unclimbed rock and ice. Ed started to lead the first new pitch. Suddenly he remembered he'd forgotten his ice ax in the rush to get started. It was down by the tent.

"What a dumb thing to do," he said to Don. "You think we should go back for it?"

"No. It would take too much time. We can make do with an icelite."

So Don and Ed took turns leading with Don's ax,

while the second man used one of our aluminum daggers for balance and purchase. Although it was awkward, it seemed to work.

To make things more unsettling, they had only five or six fixed ropes and about a dozen pitons. Matt and I had not yet been able to bring up supplies to them; they could expect us to reach the tent sometime today with more of everything, but the beautiful weather couldn't be wasted. They would go as high as they reasonably could.

Ed led the next pitch, a traverse on steep, crunchy snow, quickly and well, needing only a piton at the top to belay from. Don managed the same economy on the next, our thirty-seventh pitch, though the snow was becoming ice in which he had to chop steps. At the top of the 55-degree pitch he found a protruding block of granite, but there didn't seem to be any good cracks in it. At last he hammered a short, stubby piton in about three-quarters of an inch, tied a loop around its blade to minimize the torque if a pull should come on it, and belayed Ed up. The pitch above required another steep traverse, again on the shallow snow-ice that lay uncomfortably close to the rock beneath. Ed led it carefully. Don could see him silhouetted against the sky all the way. The sun was beginning to hit the face, and they welcomed it after their first pitches in cold shadow. To be sure, sooner or later the sun might loosen the snow, but it would be very hard to climb difficult rock without its warmth. And it looked as if they would have to climb a steep cliff very soon.

They left fixed ropes on the first three pitches, then

decided to save their few remaining ones, placing them only on the worst pitches, where they would be most helpful on the descent. Don led another pitch, their easiest yet. With excitement he realized at the top of it that he was standing beside the large smooth pillar we had noticed in the Washburn pictures, and which he knew marked the beginning of the last rock barrier. Ed led into a steep couloir, now hard blue ice in which he laboriously and precariously had to chop steps. But he reached rock on the opposite side where he could get in a good anchor. So far they had used only five pitons in five pitches—the absolute minimum, certainly fewer than they would have used had they had plenty to spare. But they had climbed fast. The snow was still solid, but the rock was warming up. It looked as if they might be able to climb the 70-degree cliff above them barehanded. They certainly couldn't climb all of it with mittens on.

Don began the cliff. At least it had a few fine, sharp-edged holds. Trying to save the pitons, he went forty feet before he put one in. It rang solidly as he pounded it—thank God for the fine rock on this route! Thirty feet above that he was faced by a blank section, un-climbable, free. He hammered in a poor piton, one that wouldn't go all the way in, but vibrated noisily as he hit it. But at last it would hold his weight, and with a stirrup he surmounted the blank stretch. Difficult as it was, the climbing exhilarated him, especially know-ing, as both Ed and he did, that above the cliff lay only the long, steep summit ice field. Don climbed into a wide chimney, moved up fifteen feet, and found the top blocked by a little ceiling. There was a way out to the left if there was even one handhold at the top of his reach. Except for a thin crack, though, there was nothing. Choosing his smallest piton, he was able to hammer it in about half an inch. He tested it cautiously, putting a carabiner through the piton's eye to hold on to. It felt insecure, but didn't budge; it would probably hold. He was forty feet above the bad piton, seventy feet above his good one. Moving delicately, putting as little weight on the piton as possible, he swung himself up and around the corner. Ed, watching tensely, saw Don step onto the snow above the highest rock. The cliff was climbed. Don quickly brought Ed up. Ed led a short pitch of crusty snow above, which seemed to lie just below the edge of something. Topping the rim, he looked ahead in amazement. The smooth expanse of the summit ice field lay above him, swooping upward at an unbroken 50-degree angle to the summit. After a month of climbing among jagged towers, inside chimneys, up enclosed couloirs, the summit ice field looked nightmarishly bare. It was like hacking one's way out of a jungle suddenly to stand on the edge of an empty desert.

It meant that they might have a chance for the summit that very day. Ed finished the pitch and brought Don up. Together they planned their attack. It was early afternoon, and going for the summit would undoubtedly require a bivouac. Four hundred feet above them stood the only bit of rock in the whole expanse, an outcrop about ten feet high. They decided to aim for it.

Four quick pitches on the unnervingly open slope brought them to it. The last fifty feet before the rock were steeper, and the sun had started to undermine the ice. They reached the rock with a feeling of relief, and agreed that the snow conditions would get worse for the next few hours. Choosing the one small ledge the rock offered, they chopped a little platform on it and pitched the tiny two-man bivouac tent Don had made. It was crowded inside, but consequently warm. Holding a stove on their laps, they could melt ice chips to make water. It was about five in the afternoon. They decided to wait for night, then go all out for the summit. It was still a long way, perhaps five more hours if things went well. But it was within reach. There was still not a cloud in the sky, no wind to disturb even a grain of snow. The afternoon sun gleamed on the mountains around them as they sat, drunk with the excitement of height, looking over the wilderness below them. For the first time they could see all of the Tokositna Glacier, even the dirty tongue sprawled on the tundra in the hazy distance, whose last ice Belmore Browne had crossed sixty years before. . . .

Matt and I had started at 11:15 A.M. from the Alley Camp. On a hunch, I had suggested that we take our down jackets and an extra lunch, as well as the ropes and pitons we were relaying up to Don and Ed. We made very good time, reaching their tent beneath the Nose in only three and a half hours. It was still early;

it seemed pointless to go down at once. We decided to climb above the Nose; at least we could put in extra rope and pitons to safeguard the route behind the leaders for their descent. We were encouraged by the fact that we couldn't hear their shouts; they must be far above.

As we were preparing to climb the Nose, Matt noticed Ed's ax beside the tent. That was very strange; why hadn't he taken it? Unable to think of a more ominous reason, we assumed he had simply forgotten it as he climbed the difficult ceiling and, once above, had decided it wasn't worth going back for. Matt put the ax in his pack so that we could give it to Ed if we caught them, or at least leave it hanging from a piton where they couldn't help finding it on their way down.

At the top of the Nose we saw the newly placed fixed rope stretching around the corner. Without much trouble we followed their steps. Matt led the first pitch, I the second. It was about 3:30 P.M.; the snow was just beginning to deteriorate in the sun. The steps they had chopped in the ice, therefore, occasionally seemed uncomfortably small; we enlarged a few of them. At the top of the thirty-seventh pitch I saw that the anchor piton was a poor one and looked around for a place to put a new one. About five minutes later I gave up and tied in to the eye of the piton. Since I wasn't sure how long the piton's blade was, I had no way of judging how far into the crack it had been hammered. But there was a fixed rope leading above to the next piton, so it seemed reasonably safe.

Matt started to lead, holding the fixed rope wrapped around his left arm. Only four feet above me he stopped on a steep ice-step to tighten his right crampon, which seemed to be coming off. As he pulled on the strap his foot slipped and he fell on top of me. Not alarmed, I put up a hand to ward off his crampon, holding him on belay with the other. As his weight hit me, I felt the snow platform I had stomped for my feet collapse. But I was tied in with only a foot or two of slack, and I knew that the anchor would catch me immediately, and I would have no trouble catching Matt a foot or two below me. Yet we were sliding suddenly, unchecked. I realized the piton must have pulled out, but wondered in a blur why the fixed rope wasn't holding me; had it come loose, too? We were falling together, gaining speed rapidly. Matt was on top of me. We began to bounce, and each time we hit I had the feeling, without any pain, that I was being hurt terribly. Everything was out of control. I was still probably holding the rope in a belay, but I could do nothing to stop us. The mountain was flashing by beneath us, and with detachment I thought, This is what it's like. . . .

Suddenly we stopped. Matt was sitting on top of me. For an instant we didn't dare breathe. Then we carefully tried to stand on the steep ice.

"Don't move yet!" I said. "We could start going again!"

Now the fear, which we hadn't had time to feel as we fell, swept over us.

"Are you all right?" Matt asked urgently.

I couldn't believe those bounces hadn't broken any bones. I could move all right and I didn't seem to be bleeding. "I think so. Are you?"

"I guess. I lost my ice ax, though."

Then I realized my glasses were missing. As I looked around I saw them balanced on the tip of my boot. I grabbed them and put them on.

"We've got to get a piton in immediately," I said.

I managed to hammer in several poor ones. We could relax a little now, but trying to relax only made us more frightened. Matt had lost the crampon he was adjusting and both mittens. I had lost the dark clip-ons to my glasses. My right crampon had been knocked off, but it hung from my ankle by the strap. We were bruised but otherwise unhurt. The fall seemed to have been selectively violent.

What had stopped us? Matt still had his hand wrapped around the fixed rope, yet we had been falling without any apparent retardation. I looked up. The fixed rope, no longer attached to the anchor I had been belaying from, still stretched in one long chain to the anchor on the next pitch beyond. We saw Matt's ax, too, planted in the ice where his fall had started. Then we saw that the climbing rope had snagged above us on a little nubbin of rock. That was apparently what had stopped us.

It was safer, at least at first, to go up than to go down. I led, soon getting a very good piton in. I traversed back into our steps. As I passed the nubbin that had caught the rope, I looked at it. It was rounded, no bigger than the knuckle of one of my fingers.

Finally I got to a safe anchor above the bad one. As Matt came up, I tried to figure out what had happened. Just after we stopped falling, I had noticed the piton dangling at my feet, still tied to me, but unconnected to the fixed rope. I realized that I had attached myself to the piton's eye, while the fixed ropes had been tied around its blade. When the piton came out, we were no longer connected to the fixed ropes, except by the grasp of Matt's left hand.

We were extremely shaken. We discussed whether to go back or go on. I wanted to go on. The accident, though it had scared us badly, shouldn't affect our general resolve, I said. I had the feeling, too, that if we went back now we might develop an overwhelming, irrational fear and never want to go above the Nose. Matt reluctantly agreed. Fortunately, I had an extra pair of mittens for him. I could get along without the dark glasses, since it was growing late; but the loss of Matt's crampon was more serious. If I led the rest of the pitches, though, enlarging the right-foot steps for him, we thought it would work.

We continued, still shaky and nervous. Now we deliberately overpitoned the route, making it as safe as was humanly possible. As we climbed, we regained confidence. Soon we no longer had Ed's and Don's fixed ropes to follow, but their steps were clear. Wondering where they had climbed the cliff, I caught sight of a fixed rope dangling. The sight was more than exciting; it was reassuring as well.

I led the cliff, marveling at the difficulties Ed and Don had overcome with only three pitons. I put in about five more. As the sun passed over Foraker, low to the west, I emerged on the summit ice field. There was still no sign of Don and Ed, but as I belayed Matt up, I heard Ed shout to us from somewhere above.

"Where are you?" I yelled back.

"In the rock outcrop!"

We couldn't see them, but hearing their voices again was thrilling. Matt and I hurried up the steep ice to join them. The conditions were at their worst now, even though it was 8:00 P.M. Twice I had to hammer rock pitons into the ice for anchors, never a dependable technique.

At last we were reunited. It was wonderful to see them. Ed said at once, "You didn't happen to bring my ice ax up, did—you did? What a couple of buddies!" Then, trying not to overstate it, we described our near-accident. Ed, especially, seemed disturbed; but the safety of numbers and the realization that now we could go to the summit together, as a rope of four, made up for all our misgivings. We ate a few candy bars as the sun set behind McKinley and the mountains faded into the dusky pallor of early night. Around 10:00 P.M. we started.

Since we had only two ropes, we had to tie in at 90-foot intervals instead of the usual 140. Don went first, I second, Matt third, while Ed brought up the rear. In order to save time, I belayed Don above me with one rope and one hand and Matt below me with the other simultaneously. It was growing dark rapidly.

Soon I could see Don only as a faint silhouette in the sky, seeming to walk toward Cassiopeia. We were getting tired; the darkness made our effort seem more private, more detached from the mountain beneath us. After five pitches, at half-past midnight, we reached the summit ridge. We could scarcely tell we were there, except by the gradual leveling of the steep slope. We knew the far side was festooned with cornices overhanging the Ruth Glacier, so we didn't go all the way up to the ridge's level crest.

Now all that remained was the quarter-mile across to the summit, a narrow, airy walkway with a 5,000-foot drop on the left and a 6,000-foot drop on the right. This was the first and only part of our climb that coincided with the French route. Although it was such a short distance to the top, we knew we couldn't afford to underestimate it, for it had taken the French four and a half hours to reach the summit from here a year and a month before. For 600 feet we moved continuously, a ghostly walk in the sky. The night seemed to muffle all sound, and I had the illusion for an instant that we were the only people alive in the world. Soon we faced two flutings, short walls of vertical snow carved and crusted by the incessant wind, which spared the ridge only a few days each year. Perhaps we had been lucky enough to hit one of them. Here it was imperative that the four of us spread as far apart as possible. Don started up toward the first fluting as I belayed from a not very solid ice ax. Traversing high, he stuck his foot through the cornice and quickly pulled it back. Through the hole he could see the dull blueness of the Ruth Glacier below. He returned to my belay spot near exhaustion from the tension and exertion of a whole day of leading. We traded places and I started for the fluting, approaching it lower. The light was returning; an orange wall of flame lit the tundra north of McKinley. I could see the contours of the nearby snow now, glimmering palely. As I neared the bottom of the first wall, I thought I saw something sticking out of the snow. I climbed over to it. Stretched tight in the air, a single, frail foot of thin rope emerged from the ice. I pulled on it, but it was stuck solid. The sight was strangely moving. It testified, in a way, both to the transience and to the persistence of man. That bit of French fixed rope was the only human thing not our own that we had found during the whole expedition. It even seemed to offer a little security. I clipped in to it although I knew it was probably weather-rotten.

It seemed best to attack the fluting high, probably even on top of the cornice. If it broke off, at least there would be the weight of the other three on the opposite side of the ridge to hold me. The snow was terrible, made more out of air than anything else. I used one of our longest aluminum daggers in my left hand, my ax in the right, trying to plant something in the snow I could hold on to. At last, by hollowing a kind of trough out of the fluting, I could half climb, half chimney up. Just beyond its top the second fluting began. Don came up to belay me for the new obstacle. It was a little harder, but with a last spurt of energy I got over it. Though things seemed to be happening quickly to me, I took a long time on each fluting, and Matt and Ed grew cold waiting at the other end of the rope. Eventually all four of us were up, however. Then there were only three pitches left, easy ones, and suddenly I stood on top, belaying the others up. The summit itself was a cornice, so we had to remain a few feet below it, but our heads stood higher.

It was 3:30 A.M. We'd been going for sixteen hours without rest. Now we were too tired even to exult. The sun had just risen in the northeast; a hundred and thirty miles away we could see Deborah, only a shadow in the sky. As Don looked at it I said, "This makes up for a lot." He nodded.

There was no one to tell about it. There was, perhaps, nothing to tell. All the world we could see lay motionless in the muted splendor of sunrise. Nothing stirred, only we lived; even the wind had forgotten us. Had we been able to hear a bird calling from some pine tree, or sheep bleating in some valley, the summit stillness would have been familiar; now it was different, perfect. It was as if the world had held its breath for us. Yet we were so tired . . . the summit meant first of all a place to rest. We sat down just beneath the top, ate a little of our lunch, and had a few sips of water. Ed had brought a couple of firecrackers all the way up; now he wanted to set one off, but we were afraid it would knock the cornices loose. There was so little to do, nothing we really had the energy for, no gesture appropriate to what we felt we had accomplished: only a numb happiness, almost a languor. We photographed each other and the views, trying even as we took the pictures to impress the sight on our memories more indelibly than the cameras could on the film. If only this moment could last, I thought, if no longer than we do. But I knew even then that we would forget, that someday all I should remember would be the memories themselves, rehearsed like an archaic dance; that I should stare at the pictures and try to get back inside them, reaching out for something that had slipped out of my hands and spilled in the darkness of the past. And that someday I might be so old that all that might pierce my senility would be the vague heart-pang of something lost and inexplicably sacred, maybe not even the name Huntington meaning anything to me, nor the names of three friends, but only the precious sweetness leaving its faint taste mingled with the bitter one of dying. And that there were only four of us (four is not many), and that surely within eighty years and maybe within five (for climbing is dangerous) we would all be dead, the last of our deaths closing a legacy not even the mountain itself could forever attest to.

We sat near the summit, already beginning to feel the cold. I got up and walked a little bit beyond, still roped, down the top of the east ridge, which someday men would also climb. From there I could see the underside of the summit cornice and tell that we had judged right not to step exactly on top. We had touched it with our ice axes, reaching out, but it might not have borne our weight.

Ed, who was normally a heavy smoker, had sworn

off for the whole expedition. Now, out of his inexhaustible pockets, he pulled three cigarettes. He had no trouble lighting them; after smoking two, though, he felt so light-headed he had to save the third. One of the things he must have looked forward to, I realized, was that ritual smoke on the summit, partly because of the surprise he knew it would cause. But that was only one of Ed's reasons for being there, a minor one. I thought then, much as I had when Matt and I sat on the glacier just after flying in, that I wanted to know how the others felt and couldn't. Trying to talk about it now would have seemed profane; if there was anything we shared, it was the sudden sense of quiet and rest. For each of us, the high place we had finally reached culminated ambitions and secret desires we could scarcely have articulated had we wanted to. And the chances are our various dreams were different. If we had been able to know each others', perhaps we could not have worked so well together. Perhaps we would have recognized, even in our partnership, the vague threats of ambition, like boats through a fog: the unrealizable desires that drove us beyond anything we could achieve, that drove us in the face of danger; our unanswerable complaints against the universe— that we die, that we have so little power, that we are locked apart, that we do not know. So perhaps the best things that happened on the summit were what we could see happening, not anything beneath. Perhaps it was important for Don to watch me walk across the top of the east ridge; for Matt to see Ed stand with a cigarette in his mouth, staring at the sun; for me to notice how Matt sat, eating only half his candy bar; for Ed to hear Don insist on changing to black-and-white film. No one else could see these things; no one else could even ask whether or not they were important. Perhaps they were all that happened.

It was getting a little warmer. We knew we had to get down before the sun weakened the snow, especially on the summit ice field. Each of us as we left took a last glance back at the summit, which looked no different than when we had come, but for the faint footprints we had left near it.

We put fixed ropes in on all the difficult pitches, refusing to let up or get careless now that we were so tired. For the same reason we didn't take dexedrine tablets, though we carried them. When we reached the bivouac tent, we split into pairs to continue down. Ed and I went first, while Don and Matt packed up the little camp before following us. The sun, high in a still perfect sky, had taken the magic out of the mountain's shapes. Only the soft early light and the tension of our expectancy could have left it as beautiful as it had been. At last, after twenty-five straight hours of technical climbing, we rappelled off the Nose and piled, all four together, into the tent.

Now we could relax at last, but the tent was far too crowded. We felt giddy, and laughed and shouted as the edge of our alertness wore off. We had brought up our pint of victory brandy—blackberry-flavored—and now indulged in a few sips, toasting everything from

Washburn to Kalispell. Each of us managed to doze off at some time or other, with someone else's foot or elbow in his face. In the afternoon it grew unbearably hot and stuffy inside, and the Nose began to drip (appropriately enough), pouring water through the roof of the tent. We cooked all our favorite delicacies, robbing the two food boxes rapaciously. By 6:00 P.M. it had started to cool again, and we saw that, finally, the weather might be turning bad, after six consecutive perfect days, a spell almost unheard of in Alaska. It was as if the storms had politely waited for us to finish our climb. We slept a little more, but still couldn't get comfortable. Around 9:00 P.M. Ed suggested that he and I go down in the night to the Alley Camp. We were still tired, but it wouldn't be a difficult descent. Once he and I got to the Camp, moreover, all four of us could rest in luxurious comfort, a sleeping bag each, room to stretch out full length, and plenty of food to wait out any storm. We dressed and were ready to go by 9:40 P.M.

8 ▲ The Accident

The snow was in poorer condition than we liked; it hadn't refrozen yet, and might not that night since a warm wind was coming in. I knew the pitches below better than Ed, having been over them five times to his one, so I tried to shout instructions to him when the route was obscure. It got to be too dark to see a full rope-length. I went down the twenty-ninth pitch, our ice-filled chimney, feeling rather than seeing the holds. But the fixed ropes helped immensely, and since I came last on the two hard pitches (twenty-ninth and twenty-seventh), Ed didn't have to worry so much about not knowing the moves. Despite the conditions, we were moving efficiently.

At the top of the twenty-sixth pitch, the vertical inside corner Don had led so well in crampons, we stopped to rappel. We stood, side by side, attached to the bottom of the fixed rope we had just used on the pitch above. In the dark, we could discern only the outlines of each other's faces. Under our feet, we felt our crampons bite the ice. Just below the little ledge we stood on, the rock shrank vertically away, and empty space lurked over the chasm below. It was too dark to see very far down. Above us, the steepest part of the face, which we had just descended, loomed vaguely in the night. Up there, on another ledge, Don and Matt were probably sleeping. Beside us, in the mild darkness, icicles dripped trickles of water that splashed on the rocks. The fixed rope was wet; here and there ice, from the splashing, had begun to freeze on it.

We didn't have an extra rope, so we untied and attached ourselves to the fixed line, setting up a rappel with the climbing rope. Ed attached a carabiner to the anchor, through which he clipped the climbing rope, so that we could pull it down from the bottom. He wrapped the rope around his body and got ready to rappel. We were tired, but were getting down with reasonable speed. It was ten minutes before midnight.

"Just this tough one," I said. "Then it's practically walking to camp."

"Yeah," Ed answered.

He leaned back. Standing about five feet from him,

I heard a sharp scraping sound. Suddenly Ed was flying backward through the air. I could see him fall, wordless, fifty feet free, then strike the steep ice below.

"Grab something, Ed!" But even as I shouted, he was sliding and bouncing down the steep ice, tangled in the rappel rope. He passed out of sight, but I heard his body bouncing below. From the route photos I knew where he had fallen; there wasn't a chance of his stopping for 4,000 feet.

Perhaps five seconds had passed. No warning, no sign of death—but Ed was gone. I could not understand. I became aware of the acute silence. All I could hear was the sound of water dripping near me. "Ed! Ed! Ed!" I shouted, without any hope of an answer. I looked at the anchor—what could have happened? The piton was still intact, but the carabiner and rope were gone with Ed. It made no sense.

I tried to shout for help to Matt and Don. But they were nearly 1,000 feet above, hidden by cliffs that deflected and snow that absorbed my voice. I realized they couldn't hear me. Even the echo of my shouts in the dark seemed tiny. I couldn't just stand there; either I must go up or I must go down. It was about an equal distance either way, but the pitches above were more difficult. I had no rope. There was no point going up, because there was nothing we could do for Ed. His body lay now, as far as anyone could ever know, on the lower Tokositna, inaccessible. An attempt even by the three of us to descend the 4,000 feet to look for him would be suicidally dangerous, especially since we would have only one rope for all of us. If I went up, I should eventually have to go down again. All it could do was add to the danger. I realized these things at the time. Yet the instinct, in my isolation, to try to join Matt and Don was so compelling that for a while I didn't even consider the other possibility. But it became obvious I had to go down.

At least the fixed ropes were still in. I used two carabiners to attach myself to them, then began to climb down the steep pitch we had started to rappel. I moved jerkily, making violent efforts, telling myself to go more slowly. But I had to use the adrenaline that was racing through me now; it was the only thing that could keep the crippling fear and grief temporarily from me.

I managed to get down the hard pitch. The snow on the Upper Park was in poor condition. I broke steps out beneath me, but held my balance with the fixed rope. I realized that I was going far too fast for safety, but slowing down was almost impossible. As I traversed to the Alley, I was sure the weak snow would break under my feet, but it held. At last I arrived at the tent. The seven pitches had taken eighteen minutes, dangerously fast. But I was there; now there was nothing to do but wait alone.

I crawled into the tent. It was full of water. Matt and I had left the back door open! In the dark I sponged it out, too tired to cry, in something like a state of shock. I took two sleeping pills and fell asleep.

In the morning I gradually woke out of a gray stupor. It seemed to be snowing lightly. I felt no sudden pang about the accident; even in sleep I must have remained aware of it. I forced myself to cook and eat a breakfast, for the sake of establishing a routine, of occupying myself. I kept thinking, *What could have happened?* The carabiner and rope were gone; nothing else had been disturbed. Perhaps the carabiner had flipped open and come loose; perhaps it had broken; perhaps Ed had clipped in, in such a way that he wasn't really clipped in at all. Nothing seemed likely. It didn't matter, really. All that mattered was that our perfect expedition, in one momentary mechanical whim, had turned into a trial of fear and sorrow for me, as it would for Matt and Don when they learned, and into sudden blankness for Ed. His death had come even before he could rest well enough to enjoy our triumph.

The time passed with terrible slowness. I knew Matt and Don would be taking their time now that it was snowing. I grew anxious for their arrival, afraid of being alone. I tried to relax, but I caught myself holding my breath, listening. Occasionally a ball of snow would roll up against the tent wall. I was sure each time that it was one of them kicking snow down from above. I would stick my head out the tent door, looking into the empty whiteness for a sign of them. My mind magnified even the sound of snowflakes hitting the tent into their distant footsteps.

I made myself eat, write in my diary, keep the tent dry, keep a supply of ice near the door. But I began to worry about Matt and Don, too. I knew there was no reason to expect them yet, but what if they had had an accident, too?

There were some firecrackers in the tent. We had

tentatively arranged on the way up to shoot them off in an emergency. I might have done that now, but there was no emergency. It would be more dangerous to communicate with them than not to, because in their alarm they might abandon caution to get down fast.

I began to wonder what I would do if they didn't come. What if I heard them calling for help? I would have to go up, yet what could I do alone? I calculated that they had at most five days' food at the Nose Camp. I had enough for twenty days at the Alley Camp. I would wait five or six days, and if there was no sign of them, I would try to finish the descent alone. At the cave I could stamp a message for Sheldon; if he flew over, he would see it. If he didn't, I would eventually start to hike out, seventy miles down an unknown glacier, across rivers, through the tundra. . . .

But these were desperate thoughts, the logical extremes of possible action I might have to take; I forced myself to consider them so that no potential course of events could lurk unrealized among my fears.

Already I had begun to miss Ed in a way separate from the shock and loneliness. I longed for his cheeriness, that fund of warmth that Matt, Don, and I lacked. I had wanted so much to relax in the tent, talking and joking with him, reliving the long summit day. I hadn't climbed with him since July 11. Now it was the last day of the month, and he was gone.

I went outside the tent only to urinate. Each time, I tied a loop around my waist and clipped in to a piton outside, not only because I was afraid but because I couldn't be sure that the sleeping pills and the shock (if it was actually shock) were not impairing my judgment or balance. I felt always tense, aware that I was waiting, minute by minute. I could think of very little but the accident; I couldn't get the sight of Ed falling, sudden and soundless, out of my head.

The snow continued to fall lightly, but the tent got warmer as the hidden sun warmed the air. In the afternoon I began to hear a high, faint whining sound. It was like nothing human, but I couldn't place it. Could it be some kind of distress signal from Matt or Don? Impossible. . . . Could it be the wind blowing through a carabiner somewhere above? But there was almost no wind. Was it even real? I listened, holding my breath, straining with the effort to define the sound. I couldn't even tell if it was above the camp or below. I sang a note of the same pitch to convince myself the sound was real. It seemed to stop momentarily, but I couldn't be sure I hadn't merely begun to ignore it. Finally I noticed that when I went outside the tent, I couldn't hear it. Therefore the sound had to come from inside. At last I found it—vaporized gas, heated by the warmth of the day, was escaping from the stove's safety valve! I felt silly but measurably relieved.

I tried to relive every moment Ed and I had had together the last day, as if doing so could somehow salvage something from the tragedy. My recollections had stuck on a remark he had made in the Nose Camp as we rested after the summit. I had told him that it had been the best day I'd ever had climbing. Ed had said, "Mine too, but I don't know if I'd do the whole thing again."

I thought he was still upset about Matt's and my near-accident, and suggested so. Ed thought a moment, then said, "No. It's not only that."

We hadn't pursued it, but his attitude had seemed strange to me. For me, there was no question but that it would have been worth doing all over again. Nor for Don. And I thought Matt would have said so, too. But Ed had climbed less than we had; perhaps he wasn't so sure that climbing was the most important thing in his life, as we would have said it was in ours.

Now his remark haunted me. The accident, ultimately inexplicable beyond its mechanical cause, which itself we would never be sure of, seemed that much more unfair in view of what Ed had said. It would have been better, fairer, perhaps, had it happened to me. Yet not even in the depth of anguish could I wish that I had died instead. And that irreducible selfishness seemed to prove to me that beyond our feeling of "commitment" there lay the barriers of our disparate self-love. We were willing to place our lives in each other's hands, but I wouldn't have died for Ed. What a joke we played on ourselves—the whole affair of mountaineering seemed a farce then. But the numbness returned; I told myself to wait, to judge it all in better perspective, months, years from now.

By that night there had still been no sign of Matt or Don. I took another sleeping pill and finally dozed off. Sometime in the night, on the edge of sleeping and waking, I had a vision of Ed stumbling, bloody, broken, up to the tent, yelling out in the night, "Why didn't you come to look for me?" I woke with a jolt, then waited in the dark for the dream to dissolve. I hadn't considered, after the first moments, trying to look for Ed's body. For me alone, without a rope, to try to descend the 4,000 feet would certainly have been suicide. Yet because there was nothing to do, and because I hadn't seen Ed's dead body, a whisper of guilt had lodged in my subconscious, a whisper that grew to Ed's shout in my nightmare.

I took a sip of water and fell asleep again. In the morning I discovered my watch had stopped. An unimportant event, it hit me with stunning force. It was as if one more proof of reality were gone, one more contact with the others, Matt and Don first of all, everyone else alive in the world eventually. I set the watch arbitrarily and shook it to get it started.

That day, August 1, dragged by as the last one had. I was no more relaxed than I had been before. The weather was good for a few minutes in the morning, then clouded up again; but at least it had stopped snowing. I felt surer now that Matt and Don would get to me, but I began to dread their arrival, for it would open the wounds of shock in them, and I would have to be the strong one, at first.

I thought of how rarely an expedition is both successful and tragic, especially a small expedition. Something like 95 per cent of the dangers in a climb such as ours lay in the ascent. But we had worked for thirty-one days, many of them dangerous, on the route without a serious injury before finally getting to the summit. Going down should have taken only two or three days, and it is usually routine to descend pitches on which fixed ropes have been left. I was reminded of the first ascent of the Matterhorn, when only hours after its conquest the climbing rope broke, sending four of Edward Whymper's seven-man party to their deaths. Then I realized that the Matterhorn had been climbed one hundred years, almost to the day, before our ascent. I thought, also, of the ascent of Cerro Torre in Patagonia in 1959, still regarded by many as the hardest climb ever done. On its descent Toni Egger, one of the best mountaineers in the world, had fallen off a cold rappel to his death, leaving only Cesare Maestri to tell of their victory. But thinking of those climbs explained ours no better. I knew that Whymper, after the Matterhorn, had been persecuted by the public, some of whom even suggested he had cut the rope. I knew that, even in an age that understands mountaineering a little better than the Victorians did, vague suspicions still shrouded the Cerro Torre expedition. But even if we could explain Ed's death to mountaineers, how could we ever explain it to those who cared more about him than about any mountain?

Around 4:00 P.M. I heard the sound of a plane, probably Sheldon's, flying near the mountain. I couldn't see anything through the mist, but perhaps his very presence meant that it was clear up above, possibly that he could see our steps leading to the summit.

Around 10:00 P.M. I thought I heard a shout. I

looked out of the tent, but saw nothing, and was starting to attribute the sound to a random noise of the
mountain, ice breaking loose somewhere or a rock falling, when suddenly Matt came in sight at the top of
the Alley. He let out a cheery yell when he saw me.
I couldn't answer, but simply stared at him. Pretty
soon Don came in sight and yelled, "How are things
down there?" I pretended I couldn't hear him. Matt
said later that they had seen our tracks from high on
the mountain and therefore known that Ed and I
hadn't completed the descent to the cave. This had
disturbed them a little, and their mood had acquired
gloominess during the treacherous last descent, on steps
covered by new snow, using ice-coated fixed ropes, once
belaying in a waterfall that had frozen their parkas
stiff. But as they approached, Matt had seen my head
poking out of the tent and for an instant had thrown
off his worries. Yet my silence made him uneasy again;
then, before he got to the tent, he saw that there was
only one pack beside it. Then I said, "Matt, I'm alone."

He belayed Don all the way down before either of
us said anything to him. When Matt told him, Don
stood there frozen momentarily, looking only at the
snow. Then, in a way I cannot forget, he seemed to
draw a breath and swallow the impact of the shock.
He said, "All right. Let's get inside the tent." His
voice, calm as ever, was heavy with a sudden fatigue.
But once they knew, once I saw that they were taking it
without panic, being strong, I felt an overwhelming
gratitude toward them: out of my fear, an impulse
like love.

9 ▲ Remnants

We spent a crowded, uncomfortable night. The tent platform had begun to slope downhill, and it was too small for all of us. We had planned to finish the descent when the weather became good. But the next day it was storming, probably the worst day we had had. We began to worry about the pitches below getting unclimbably dangerous; perhaps even the fixed ropes might be buried. Although it was only August 2, winter was arriving: the days were growing not only shorter but noticeably colder.

We spent most of the day waiting for a let-up, but

our crowded situation was too unpleasant. As long as we had the rest of the descent before us we could not relax. We decided to go in the late afternoon despite the storm. We got dressed and moved outside the tent. A bitter wind whistled across the ridge, chilling us at once. We had a difficult time taking down the tent, because we got in each other's way trying to maneuver around the platform while staying tied in to our pitons. Moreover, the tent's back corner had frozen into the ice. At last we half chopped, half ripped it out. Our hands lost their feeling almost immediately when we had to take our mittens off; our toes grew numb after the first few minutes.

We were ready to leave by 7:30 P.M. We thought it should take about two hours to get down to the cave. In good weather we had done it in little more than one hour. Now we faced the problem of descending, three on a rope, pitches that were made for only two. Since Matt had just one crampon, he had to go in the middle. Don started off, while I waited to descend last.

The snow conditions were terrible, by far the worst we had yet run into. A full foot of loose powdery snow overlay our steps; often the steps themselves had melted out, leaving only the slick surface of the ice beneath. We went continuously at first, but at a pace slower than a snail's. Don had to rechop steps under the snow, reaching awkwardly down with his ax. The fixed ropes were coated with ice, sometimes in a solid sheath a quarter-inch thick. Moreover, since we were only seventy feet apart, two of us were often relying

▲ 137

on the same section of fixed rope at the same time, threatening to pull each other off. Matt, despite his missing crampon, had to use the ropes as little and as gently as possible, because I, coming last, could not afford to fall, and Don wouldn't have been able to replace the steps without holding on to something.

But we seemed to move all right on the comparatively easy, rock-free pitches of the Lower Park. At least, once we got going we were all three in motion most of the time, and our feet and hands began to warm up a little.

On the thirteenth pitch, the one which joined the Stegosaur to the Lower Park, Don suddenly shouted, "Falling!" Matt and I braced ourselves, but the pull never came. Don had managed to hold himself with the fixed rope. The pitch was in terrible shape. We had to traverse awkwardly on steep ice that was coated with a rime-frost that looked solid until stepped on. Matt fell at the same spot Don had, but caught himself the same way. Gamely, he went back to rechop the steps so that I might get down safely. When I reached the spot, I found the fixed rope was of no use for balance, but I had to hold on to it in case of a slip. Even with the improved steps, I came as near falling as I ever have without coming off. Matt and Don had stopped to belay me. There were only three and a half more pitches above the rappel, but we realized we had to belay each one of them carefully. The rock added a factor of difficulty that made it too dangerous to travel continuously. First we tried tying Matt in only five feet above Don, while I belayed both of them from a solid stance. They crept down the twelfth pitch. I got very cold again, and begged the rope to pay out faster, since that was all I could see of their progress. Finally one of them yelled, "On belay!" and I could descend. The pitch was far more difficult than it ever had been on the way up. I was afraid that the fixed rope might have weathered enough to be dangerously weak, but I had to rely on it anyway. When I reached them, Don and Matt said the system was no good. They had kept getting in each other's way, pulling each other off; it was an impossible effort to co-ordinate their movements.

We moved Matt back to the middle of the rope. I went first, while Don, already quite cold, had to stand in the same spot for a much longer time to belay us ahead. It was starting to get really dark; it must have been near midnight. The darkness intensified my nervousness. Even in the best psychological state, that kind of climbing would make one very uneasy. Now, under the pall of fear Ed's death had imposed, the descent became, for me at least, a nightmarish episode. In addition, the cold and the biting wind increased our clumsiness and tended to isolate us further, because it was hard to hear our shouts against the wind and unpleasant to hold one's face into it in order to watch. Within a few minutes, it was too dark to see each other very far apart anyway.

I was glad at first to lead, to be rid of the responsibility of coming last. But I began to appreciate what a job it was to replace the steps. We couldn't take off our mittens, but I needed to scrape and chop the snow off holds whose location I only dimly recalled. Finally I would get to a piton, and Matt could start moving. It was still a while before Don could begin, though. When he shouted, his voice shook with the cold.

It grew almost pitch dark. The lower we got on the mountain, the darker it got, and the enclosed recesses between the towers of the Stegosaur shut out the faint light from the north, if not the wind.

At last we were getting down. We decided to go continuously again, for we were so cold we couldn't stand the immobility of belaying, and the rope now passed over fingers of rock between us that would catch a fall as well as would any belay we might make. At one point Don and I stood on top of two towers while Matt climbed in the gap between. The rope stuck; I yelled at Matt, but there was no answer. Don and I could hear each other's shouts perfectly, but Matt seemed oblivious. I started to go back for him, but at last Matt heard Don and answered. His voice sounded as far away as if he were on a different mountain.

I finally got within a few feet of the top of the rappel, but I couldn't reach it. Matt was stuck in an incredible tangle at the last piton. I heard him swearing at the ropes, then suddenly a frightened cry from Don as he fell. Again, the fixed rope caught him, but he couldn't find any of the steps. I felt annoyed because we were climbing so poorly. But it was so cold, and I felt the tiredness seeping even into the edge of nervousness I had known for three days. We were almost down; then there would be no more hard climbing. For eighteen days we had hung every minute, over that abyss, never less than 3,000 feet above its hidden floor: the place where Ed's body now lay.

At last Matt got the tangle straightened out. I reached the piton and belayed them down. We were together again. It almost seemed too great an effort to tie the two ropes together so that we could pull them down after we had rappelled. The rope we had left there had frozen in at the bottom so that we could scarcely pull up enough slack to pass around our bodies. But finally we managed to set the thing up. I stepped over the side of the ridge with a conscious sense of relief and quickly rappelled down, knocking the ice off the rope we had left. Matt and Don followed. Then we pulled the ropes down, cutting ourselves off for good from our route, from the far, frozen summit. We staggered back to the cave, arriving at 3:30 A.M. It had taken us eight hours to descend what we had expected to complete in two. It was the day of climbing I should least ever want to repeat.

We found the cave shrunk in size, but otherwise unchanged. The storm continued for three days. We went outside around noon on the third to stamp a sign, "Fly out," in the snow. Sheldon would see this if he flew over, we were pretty sure. There was no emergency now, no reason to call for help. If Sheldon didn't see our sign within ten days or so, we would begin to hike out.

We saw no point in searching for Ed's body. Any search we could make, even plane-assisted, would be dangerous. We would have to scour the bottom of a 6,000-foot avalanche chute, down which constantly spilled rocks and ice. After the five days of storm, his body was likely to be covered by new snow, and the chances were good that that snow wouldn't melt before winter. The body, for all we knew, had been crushed and torn in the fall. We did not want to offend its dignity by salvaging a mutilated, unrecognizable corpse. All that was mortal of Ed would freeze into an unknown glacier. Within a year there would be no part of him near its surface. Gradually the remnants of his being would sink within the Tokositna, locked in unfathomable ice. None of our words would ever stir the air above his tomb; never would anyone in that place lie about why he had died. No one would ever say there that it was right. If the unconcerned glacier should someday spill Ed's body out on the gravel bar at its mouth, rocks would still cover it; no one would ever know. Mysteries lie with Ed; but the most important of them, perhaps, could not be solved. Ed kept a diary. He had written more than a hundred pages in it in red ink, but it fell with him. That diary might have offered some clue to him, some clue to the urge that he, who made things come so easily, who understood people so well and cared about them, could have felt for an unwitnessable challenge in an inhuman place. But he had never been at rest within himself; he struggled to believe, to explain his fears and joys. The diary wouldn't have answered for those who loved him the pained question, "Why did he have to go there?"

But for Matt, Don, and me there was all of life to anticipate. We wanted to get back, but we dreaded it, too. I could picture, even then, the reception we had to expect from those who had last seen us, exuberant and eager, going off (for all some of them knew) on a pleasant summer outing. I knew even then the taste of transmitted grief that would be our duty. Already I heard the stunned, empty silence over the phone from Pennsylvania, saw the bloodshot eyes drained of hope, felt the friend's stifled wince. A remark Ed's father had made when we had stopped at their house in early June stuck in my mind now. He had said, "It's hard for you boys to understand how parents can worry about this kind of thing." I had simply agreed—it *was* hard for us to understand. Now it was tragically easier.

In the snow cave we could relax, in a sense. We no longer had to hold on to something when we went outside the tent; we no longer felt the threat of empty space beneath us. But in the absence of the tension that had bound us together, a dull feeling of loss set in. We had been robbed not only of Ed, but of all but a few hours of exultation, and would never again recall our triumph with pleasure unmitigated by pain. Now there was only another wait. To make things worse, we began to feel some of the antagonisms which our common dependence had, for the last two weeks, obliterated. We couldn't agree on a few things. I wanted to hike out in eight days or so; Don preferred to wait as long as we could. Don wanted to climb the little peak west of Huntington to get pictures of the route. I had no enthusiasm for the idea and would have felt fear on the ridge again. Matt was indifferent, but agreed to accompany Don if there was time and good weather. Don wanted to arrange, if possible, to have more food dropped in to continue climbing in our basin. I wanted to get out to face notifying Ed's parents, and Matt had to get out for a job commitment. We had talked the accident dry. All our conversation could do now was attempt to recover the sense of joy we had begun to feel as we rested at the Nose Camp after the summit. We were able, in our few days in the cave, to regain a sense of pride. I felt a strong passion, a loyalty, toward our accomplishment, but I knew it wasn't joy. We wasted time methodically, waiting for Sheldon.

On August 6 the weather cleared. We spent most of the day outside in the sun. We hoped for Sheldon, but knew the chances were good he wouldn't fly by. After all, he had been over only once since July 20, even during the long spell of good weather we had had. The new snow had plastered our route, making it look cold and splendid. In the early evening the sun lit high, ribbed clouds above McKinley, and cast a brown warmth on the rock of the face, reflected in ghostly radiance on the shadowed floor of the glacier. Never had the mountain seemed more beautiful, not even in its first untouched magic. Sheldon didn't come, however. As it got dark, we lit the few candles we had brought and set them up in the snow cave to read and write by. When I went outside, I could see the warm glow diffused through the snow of the cave's roof, and I felt an old, childish fear of the dark. The cave seemed the only island of safety in a limitless sea of night.

After we extinguished the candles, I lay awake thinking. I was trying to imagine how I could tell Ed's parents. I thought of the things that, sooner or later, people would say about Ed's death, as attempts at consolation. There were three things, especially, that would be said, things that had been said before, by me as well as others, about men who had been killed mountaineering; but now, none of them seemed to offer real consolation. It would be said that Ed died doing what he enjoyed most, that his last conscious moments were happy ones. But he did not want to die; every part of him that was aware he was falling did not want that to be, but was powerless. There was never enough happiness to last as long as we would have it. It would be said that the way he died was somehow "right." But he did not have to die; to die young is never right. It would be said that, at least, he never had time to feel pain or even fear. But, though I could not have wanted Ed to die suffering, dying without pain or fear seems to me the equivalent of living without joy. Let us be aware of our end, because life is all we have. Yet, though I could not find consolation in these thoughts, and knew they would be little consolation to his parents, I could not rid my mind of some image of beauty connected with Ed's death, as if his fall without a sound had owned, for an instant, a freedom no one ever knew in life.

At 4:00 A.M. I woke, hearing the faint hum of an

airplane. I put my boots on and ran out of the cave. It was Sheldon. Don and Matt, awake now also, joined me as we tried to point at our sign in the snow. Sheldon seemed to see it, acknowledged us by circling, then dropped a note. It landed in the crevasse below camp, but we roped up and went to get it. He instructed us to proceed to the floor of the glacier. We packed rapidly, then left the cave, looking back as we descended the icefall for the last time. A few hours later Sheldon returned, landing easily on the hard glacier. Matt and I got in the plane first. In a second load he could pick up Don and the rest of our equipment. Sheldon had seen our tracks to the summit five days before, and Matt and Don in the Nose Camp, but he had no idea that anything had gone wrong. He couldn't quite believe Ed's death. We made several passes near the bottom of the avalanche chute, but could see no sign of anything human. Then we headed out over the tundra.

Sheldon kept saying, "Boy, that's rough. What happened?" All I could do was explain the facts of the accident. I couldn't explain beyond that; I couldn't tell him the urgency of our happiness before. Huntington faded behind us; I couldn't explain. We had spent forty days alone there, only to come back one man less, it seemed. We had found no answers to life: perhaps only the room in which to look for them.

In Talkeetna the grass smelled damp and sweet. Flies swarmed, buzzing around us as we put down our packs, and the air blazed with fireweed.

Glossary

aid or direct aid — any sort of climbing that uses mechanical means (pitons, slings, stirrups) for holds or balance, instead of merely for safety.

belay — to secure one's partner against possible fall by passing the rope around the body.

bivouac tent — a two-man tent, little bigger than two men's bodies, that can be pitched on the slightest of ledges and the steepest of slopes, for a minimal camp; usually used in a final assault.

carabiner — a metal, oval snap-link that attaches the climbing rope to the piton.

chimney — an unusually steep, narrow gully.

climbing rope — the main rope, connecting a pair of climbers.

col — a gap in a ridge; a pass.

continuous climbing — both climbers moving together, roped, but without belay.

cornice — an overhanging lip of snow, formed along the top of a ridge by the wind.

couloir — a steep gully, usually filled with ice or snow.

crampons — metal spikes attached to the sole of the boot, for use on ice or hard snow.

expansion bolts — a nail or screw sleeve that is driven into the rock by means of hand drill and hammer; used as a last resort where there are no natural cracks adequate for pitons.

fixed ropes — ropes left in place to facilitate load-carrying and reclimbing a pitch.

free climbing — climbing without reliance on pitons; opposed to "aid" climbing.

ice ax — the ice climber's chief tool: a wooden or metal shaft about 2½ feet long, whose head has a pointed metal pick on one end, a flat adze on the other; it looks much like a miner's pick.

icefall — a steep, crevassed section of glacier.

icelite — a long, pointed, barbed, L-section aluminum ice piton, invented by Don Jensen specifically for Alaskan conditions; especially useful where the ice is too rotten to hold a shorter ice screw.

ice screw — a type of piton, with a corkscrew blade, that is screwed, rather than hammered, into an ice cliff.

pitch — one rope's length on the mountain.

piton — a metal peg hammered into cracks in the rock; a carabiner is attached to the head, or eye, of the piton, and the climbing rope is clipped into the carabiner, thus reducing the length of the leader's possible fall.

prusik — a means of climbing a rope that has been left in place on a steep pitch; waist- and foot-loops are tied to the main rope with a prusik knot, which slides freely up or down normally but grips and holds when one's weight is put on it.

rappel — to descend by sliding down a rope that has been attached to a piton or prong of rock.

stirrup — a three- or four-step rope ladder made of nylon webbing attached to a piton in direct-aid climbing, when there are no possible natural holds; by using several in sequence, the climber can climb pitch after pitch without a natural hold.

Appendices

Appendix I

Route Description

PITCH #	TERRAIN	LENGTH (*Feet*)	NCCS RATING*	DATE FIRST LED	LED BY
1	ice & snow (*through cornice*)	90	I3	July 5	Don & Matt
2	ice & snow & rock	120	I2, F3	July 6	Don
3	snow & rock	90	I1, F4	July 6	Dave
4	snow & rock & verglas	40	I1, F5, A1	July 6	Don
5	snow & ice	140	I4	July 7	Ed
6	rock & snow	135	I1, F4	July 7	Matt
7	rock & snow	120	I2, F3	July 10	Dave
8	rock & snow	130	I1, F4	July 10	Don
9	rock & snow	140	I2, F3	July 10	Dave
10	rock & snow	140	I1, F4	July 11	Matt
11	rock & snow	140	I2, F5	July 11	Don
12	rock & snow	120	I1, F5	July 11	Matt
13	rock & snow & ice	110	I3, F3	July 11	Don
14	snow	135	I1	July 11	Dave
15	snow	130	I1	July 11	Dave
16	snow & rock	140	I2, F3	July 11 & 16	Ed & Dave
17	snow & rock	140	I1, F3	July 16	Dave
18	snow & rock & ice	130	I1, F3	July 16	Ed

CAMP I (*ALLEY*)

19	snow	80	I1	July 16	Matt
20	snow & ice & rock	130	I2	July 16	Matt

* The NCCS (or National Climbing Classification System) is a widespread, standardized system for rating the difficulty of pitches on a climb. The F number indicates the difficulty of the free rock climbing on the pitch (from the easiest F1 to the hardest F10); the A number indicates the difficulty of the direct aid (A1 to A5). By analogy with the A rating, I have included an I rating for the difficulty of the ice or snow climbing on a pitch (I1 easiest through I5 hardest).

PITCH #	TERRAIN	LENGTH (Feet)	NCCS RATING*	DATE FIRST LED	LED BY
21	snow & rock	120	I2	July 16	Ed
22	snow	130	I1	July 16	Matt
23	snow	130	I1	July 16	Ed
24	snow	110	I1	July 16	Matt

CAMP II (*TEMPORARY*)

PITCH #	TERRAIN	LENGTH (Feet)	NCCS RATING*	DATE FIRST LED	LED BY
25	snow & rock	90	I1	July 16	Ed
26	ice & rock	100	I2, F8	July 20	Don
27	ice & rock	120	I2, F7	July 20	Ed
28	snow & ice & rock	60	I1, F3	July 20	Ed
29	snow & ice & rock	130	I2, F6, A1	July 25 & 26	Dave & Matt
30	snow & rock	140	I1, F5	July 26	Dave
31	snow & rock	100	I1, F4	July 26	Matt
32	snow & rock & ice	90	I1, F4	July 26	Dave
33	snow & ice	110	I2	July 26	Matt
34	snow	70	I1	July 26	Dave

CAMP III (*NOSE*)

PITCH #	TERRAIN	LENGTH (Feet)	NCCS RATING*	DATE FIRST LED	LED BY
35	rock	70	F5, A2	July 26	Matt
36	rock & ice & snow	120	I2, F3	July 29	Ed
37	snow	130	I2	July 29	Don
38	snow	130	I1	July 29	Ed
39	snow	120	I1	July 29	Don
40	snow & ice	120	I2	July 29	Ed
41	rock & ice	140	I2, F6, A1	July 29	Don
42	snow	130	I3	July 29	Ed
43	snow	140	I1	July 29	Don
44	snow & ice	120	I2	July 29	Ed
45	snow & rock	60	I1, F3	July 29	Don

CAMP IV (*BIVOUAC*)

PITCH #	TERRAIN	LENGTH (Feet)	NCCS RATING*	DATE FIRST LED	LED BY
46	rock & snow	90	I2, F5	July 29	Don
47	snow & ice	80	I1	July 29	Don

150 ▲

PITCH #	TERRAIN	LENGTH (*Feet*)	NCCS RATING*	DATE FIRST LED	LED BY
48	snow	80	I1	July 29	Don
49	snow	80	I1	July 29	Don
50	snow	80	I1	July 29	Don

600' UNBELAYED CLIMBING

51	snow	80	I1	July 30	Dave
52	snow	70	I4	July 30	Dave
53	snow	50	I4	July 30	Dave
54	snow	80	I1	July 30	Dave
55	snow	80	I1	July 30	Dave
56	snow	50	I1	July 30	Dave

SUMMIT

Appendix II

Occupation of Camps — ASCENT:

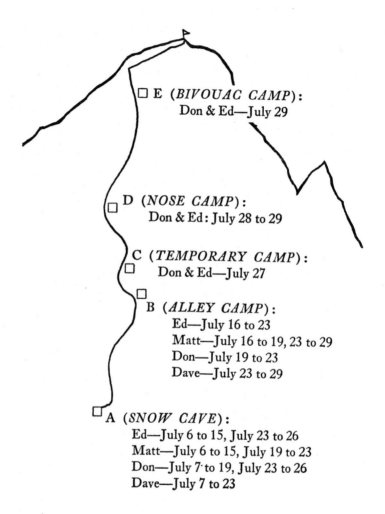

E (*BIVOUAC CAMP*):
   Don & Ed—July 29

D (*NOSE CAMP*):
   Don & Ed: July 28 to 29

C (*TEMPORARY CAMP*):
   Don & Ed—July 27

B (*ALLEY CAMP*):
   Ed—July 16 to 23
   Matt—July 16 to 19, 23 to 29
   Don—July 19 to 23
   Dave—July 23 to 29

A (*SNOW CAVE*):
   Ed—July 6 to 15, July 23 to 26
   Matt—July 6 to 15, July 19 to 23
   Don—July 7 to 19, July 23 to 26
   Dave—July 7 to 23

Occupation of Camps. — DESCENT:

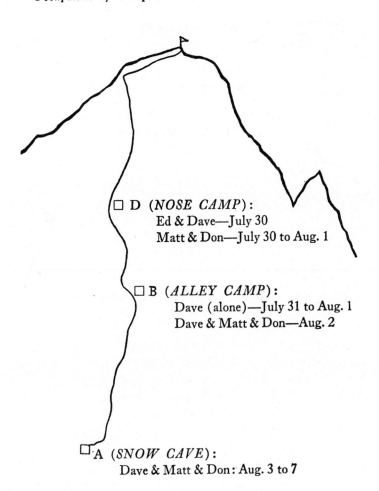

□ D (*NOSE CAMP*):
  Ed & Dave—July 30
  Matt & Don—July 30 to Aug. 1

□ B (*ALLEY CAMP*):
  Dave (alone)—July 31 to Aug. 1
  Dave & Matt & Don—Aug. 2

□ A (*SNOW CAVE*):
  Dave & Matt & Don: Aug. 3 to 7

▲ 153

Appendix III

Personal Equipment

Each Member Carried:

pack-frame, pack-sack, and pack straps
ice ax
snowshoes
crampons
sleeping bag (at least 3¼ lbs. of down)
"ensolite" rubber sleeping pad (better than an air mattress)
boots (either double boots or heavy single boots)
overboots (nylon, with canvas bottoms)
spare boot laces
gaiters (anklets to keep out snow)
socks (both heavy wool and light)
pants (Air Force "inner flight" pants)
undershorts
long johns
string-net shirt
T-shirt
heavy wool shirt
down vest and/or sweater(s)
down jacket with hood
wind parka
balaclava (a wool head mask)
mittens (light and heavy, some down-filled)
goggles or clip-on dark glasses
hard-hat (motorcycle helmet)
waist-loop
piton hammer

raincoat (plastic)
eating bowl
spoon
knife
water bottle
day-pack (light, close-fitting)
sunburn cream
toothbrush and toothpaste or powder
camera and film
diary and pencils
paperback books
plastic bags to keep personal items dry
hat

Appendix IV

2 two-man tents
rain flies (plastic) for the tents
bivouac tent
extra ice ax
extra pair of crampons
3 stoves
6 gallons white gas
matches
stove repair materials
8 assorted pots
2 snow shovels
4 climbing ropes (150' long, ⅜" in diameter, nylon)
7000' fixed rope (¼ or 5⁄16" in diameter, nylon and manila)
110 rock pitons
20 ice screws
10 ice pitons
40 icelites (special barbed aluminum ice pitons)
expansion bolt kit (for aid climbing where there are no piton cracks)
2 spare piton hammers
maps, aerial photographs (Washburn)
candles
2 head-lamps
binoculars
willow wands (bamboo stakes for marking the route on the open glaciers)
60 carabiners (metal snap-links connecting the piton to the rope)
slings and stirrups (made of nylon webbing)

parachute cord (⅛″ diameter nylon cord used for many pur-
poses)
repair kit
medical kit
280 man-days of food, packaged in plastic bags by meal
"victory brandy" (half pint blackberry brandy)
football
Monopoly game